It's another Quality Book from CGP

This book is for anyone studying _Of Mice and Men_ at GCSE.

Studying English texts can give you a real headache,
but happily this CGP book makes your life just a little bit easier.
We've crammed in absolutely everything you'll need to write about
— and there are even handy tips on essay skills to top it all off.

And it's also got some daft bits in to try and make the whole
experience at least vaguely entertaining for you.

What CGP is all about

Our sole aim here at CGP is to produce the highest quality
books — carefully written, immaculately presented and
dangerously close to being funny.

Then we work our socks off to get them out to you
— at the cheapest possible prices.

CONTENTS

BEFORE YOU START (EASY)

Write Amazing Essays 1
Cartoon of "Of Mice and Men" 2

SECTION 1 — DISCUSSION OF CHAPTERS (EASY)

Chapter 1 — A hot evening 4
Chapter 2 — Arrival and Introductions 6
Chapter 3 — It's a Dog's Life 8
Chapter 4 — Curley's Wife Spoils Things 10
Chapter 5 — A Dead Girl and a Dead Dream 12
Chapter 6 — George Kills His Best Friend 14
Revision Summary 16

SECTION 2 — CHARACTERS (OKAY)

George 17
Lennie 19
Carlson 21
Curley 22
Crooks 23
Whit 24
Slim 25
Curley's Wife 26
Candy 27
Revision Summary 28

SECTION 3 — THEMES (A BIT TRICKY)

Ranch Life 29
Shooting Candy's Dog 30
Hands 31
Names and Titles 32
The Battle of the Sexes 33
Loneliness 34
Doomed to Failure 35
Dreams 36
Why George Kills Lennie 37
Interpreting Things 38
Revision Summary 39

SECTION 4 — BACKGROUND STUFF (PRETTY HARD)

The Structure 40
The Language 41
Cool Background Stuff 42
The World in the 1930s 43
Revision Summary (and final exam tip) 44
Index 45

Published by Coordination Group Publications Ltd.

Editor:
Charley Darbishire

Contributors:
Kerry Kolbe
Peter Needham
Katherine Reed
Chrissy Williams

ISBN: 978 1 84146 114 4
Groovy website: www.cgpbooks.co.uk
Jolly bits of clipart from CorelDRAW®
Printed by Elanders Hindson Ltd, Newcastle upon Tyne.
Based on the classic CGP style created by Richard Parsons.

Text, design, layout and original illustrations
© Coordination Group Publications Ltd. 2002
All rights reserved.

Write Amazing Essays

I know you've written a zillion essays before. But read this page anyway.

Write Down a Plan of Your Essay Before You Start

Planning is important because it gets a lot of the tricky thinking out of the way. Before you start writing your essay you should:

> 1) Decide how you're going to answer the question.
> 2) Jot down a plan of the points you want to make.
> 3) Make sure you've got enough points for the whole essay.
> 4) Organise the points so they flow on from each other.

You should spend about five minutes planning your essay in an exam. Don't bother writing the plan in proper sentences — it'd waste time.

It's important to plan coursework essays too — you've got more time so the marker will expect your essay to be well thought out.

And after that line of writing, I think I'll have another line...

Structure your Essay

Your essay should be structured like this:

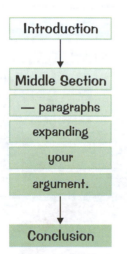

Introduction

↓

Middle Section

— paragraphs

expanding

your

argument.

↓

Conclusion

1) Your **INTRODUCTION** should give a brief answer to the question you're writing about. Make it clear how you are going to tackle the topic. Don't agonise over wording — it's OK to write, "This essay is going to argue that..."

2) The **MIDDLE SECTION** of your essay should explain your answer in detail and give evidence to back it up. Write a paragraph for each point you make. Start the paragraph by making the point, then back it up with evidence — examples from *Of Mice and Men*.

3) Always write a **CONCLUSION** — a paragraph at the end of your essay that:

   i) Sums up the most important facts and ideas in your essay.
   ii) Gives your opinion about the topic.
   iii) Argues the same thing as the rest of your essay — don't change your opinion at the last minute.

Check Everything at the End

You've got to check your essay for mistakes — in an exam, save a good five minutes for this.

1) Check that your essay includes: an introduction and conclusion that agree with each other, all the points from your original plan, and evidence to back them up.
2) If you want to get rid of something just cross it out. Don't scribble over it.
3) If you've left stuff out write it in a separate section at the end of the essay. Put a star (*) next to both the extra writing and the place you want it to go.

Don't forget to check your spelling and punctuation.

Essays essays essays...

Yup — a bit dull I know, but darned useful, even if I do say so myself. Whether it's coursework or an exam, you're going to need to know how to write a corking essay. Oh yes.

JOHN STEINBECK'S "OF MICE AND MEN"

 George Lennie Candy The Boss Curley

Chapter One — A hot evening

The book starts with George and Lennie resting by a river. It's the end of a hot day.

> 1) George and Lennie arrive at a pool of the Salinas river in California. They're described to us.
> 2) George finds Lennie has a dead mouse he's been petting.
> 3) The "bad thing" in Weed is mentioned (see page 8).
> 4) George and Lennie talk about getting a farm of their own with rabbits which will let them "live off the fatta the lan'". This is THE DREAM.

NoooOOOOOOOoooooOOO

George and Lennie are Long-term Companions

1) George leads the way. Lennie willingly follows — copying him.
2) They are very different — George is small-featured and slim, Lennie is bulky. Lennie lumbers along like a bear, and then plunges into the stream like an animal.
3) George is in a bad mood with Lennie. They've had a tough few days. Lennie just thinks of the present — so he's happy and refreshed.
4) They have a secret. They are on the run from Lennie's "bad thing" he did in Weed.
5) Lennie keeps asking George loads of questions — he's like a demanding child.
6) George is irritated by the questions — he's like a harassed and impatient parent.

Look at pages 17-20 for more about Lennie and George

The Future is Uncertain — there are Several Possibilities

1) George has decided to delay getting to their destination — so they can rest a bit.
2) Lennie would be happy in the future just to have a fresh mouse to pet.
3) George says he would be happy without Lennie. He'd have lots of food, drink and girls. He seems to be using these dreams to make Lennie feel guilty — the way parents can do. It's not clear whether or not he actually believes he would be happy without him.
4) Lennie offers to leave — he'd find a cave and a mouse, lie in the sun and be happy. He seems to be wanting to make George feel guilty too.

The Dream — They're gonna live "off the fatta the lan'"

George talks about their plans — they'll have a small farm together with animals and crops. Lennie will get to look after the rabbits. They've talked about this before, many times. This is their dream — and this and other dreams keep coming up in the book. (see page 36 for more about them)

I'm not sure whether I'm meant to be cute or ominous in this graphic...

Lennie's a .... bear — why the long paws...

Lennie's movements are often described as those of a bear. And other animals too: we're told he uses "his big paw", that he snorts "like a horse", and behaves "like a terrier". Steinbeck obviously wants us to be aware of Lennie's wildness, strength and loyalty to George. I think I want to be a badger.

Chapter One — A hot evening

There is no Stability or Certainty in their Lives

Things aren't all rosey and hunkydory though. No siree...

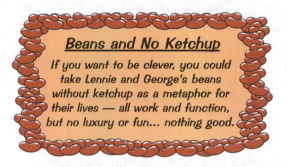

Beans and No Ketchup
If you want to be clever, you could take Lennie and George's beans without ketchup as a metaphor for their lives — all work and function, but no luxury or fun... nothing good.

1) George is anxious. They are on the run. They're between jobs and sleeping rough.
2) They're hot, tired and hungry. And there's no ketchup for the beans.
3) George finds fault with everything about his friend — the way he drinks, his dead mouse, his demands for food and chat and the fact he can't remember things.

Lennie is in some ways better off than George. He lives in the present. At the moment he's happy. George however bears the burden of knowing that they're homeless and friendless.

It's Beautiful by the pool — but also a bit Creepy

1) It's a refuge for the men after a long journey — sheltered and safe.
2) It's a beautiful spot and it's a lovely time of day ("evening of a hot day").
3) There are animals everywhere — the coyote, carp, dog, watersnake, dove and heron.
4) It's a place alive with noises of wildlife.
5) It's a place of contrasts — the wild rocky hillside and the more homely and overgrown riverside.

It's going to be "nice sleeping here" according to George. But it's a bit of creepy place.
There's something not quite right. Night is falling and George tells Lennie to let the fire die out.

This is important because it shows that not everything is as good as is seems.
There are troubles hiding in the background.

This Chapter is a Rollercoaster Ride

1) One moment George is shouting at Lennie, the next he's comforting him. One moment he's wishing he was without Lennie, the next looking into the flames of the fire — ashamed of what he's just said.
2) George only briefly seems to believe in their paradise farm. But talking about it helps them both to relax.
3) George is aware of the dangers ahead (you could say he's almost resigned to them). He makes Lennie memorise the place they're at and promise to come there if there's trouble.
4) They seem to end the evening on a good note talking about the rabbits — they seem happy even though Lennie has to be told to shut up.

That Ronan Keating was SUCH a philsopher...

LIFE

All the ingredients are now in place for excitement and drama:

1) Contrasting and conflicting characters.
2) Hints of a dark and difficult past.
3) Two people braced for an uncertain future.

Lennie's Dead Mouse Thing
The mouse is Steinbeck warning us about what might happen. Lennie has killed something without meaning to — George says "you always killed 'em". It's happened before, and it could happen again.

All beans and no ketchup make Jack a dull boy...

There's a parental theme to George and Lennie's relationship — you can see it from both sides.
George always ends up with the responsibility even though it's Lennie who gets them into trouble.
Thing is, if you started telling Lennie off for bad things he might kill you — cos he's a raving loon.

Chapter Two — Arrival and Introductions

Lennie and George arrive at the ranch, and all the characters are introduced to us, one by one.

> 1) George and Lennie meet Candy, the swamper (handyman).
> 2) The boss walks into the bunkhouse. He's a bit aggressive and doesn't like George speaking for Lennie. He thinks George is getting something from Lennie... maybe taking his wages.
> 3) Curley (the boss's son) walks in, and takes a dislike to Lennie — Curleys's mean and he's trouble.
> 4) Curley's wife is introduced. She's tarty — Lennie likes her and thinks she's "purty" (pretty).
> 5) Slim enters the bunkhouse. He thinks Lennie and George travelling together is okay.
> 6) Carlson introduces himself. He's big, dumb, and wants to kill Candy's stinking dog.

Lennie and George get an Edgy Welcome

It's too late to work the morning shift on the farm. The first thing they get is a spot of lunch.

There's an edginess throughout this section. The atmosphere is at times tense. Lennie and George are in a new workplace with new workmates. Some are more friendly than others — Candy is welcoming, but Curley certainly isn't.

All the Action in Chapter Two happens in the Bunkhouse

Rollin' rollin' rollin',
Keep those doggies movin'

1) Everyone has his own bed and his own small cupboard.
2) Everyone has a few possessions. Some have lotions and medicines too.
3) Everyone seems to have a few magazines — "Western magazines ranch men love to read and scoff at and secretly believe".
   It's important to be able to relax, and dream of a better life.
4) In the middle there's a table for playing cards — with boxes to sit on.

The boss is a right Grumpy so and so...

George and Lennie arrive late. This has made the boss pretty angry. Candy says the boss "give the stable buck hell" — that's the guy in charge of the horses. He gets all the grief because he's black.

We also learn that the boss:
1) is sometimes a decent boss — he gave a gallon of whisky to the men at Christmas.
2) wears heeled cowboy boots with spurs on them — a sign of his power and status.
3) likes to show he's the boss. He interrogates George and Lennie — he's really aggressive. Then carefully logs their arrival in his time-book. He's on a bit of a power trip.

And his Son is Worse...

After the father has left, his son (Curley) then marches in — wearing heeled boots, like his dad.

1) He quizzes Lennie and George again, in a generally aggressive way.
2) He looks them up and down, and flexes his muscles going into a fighting crouch.
3) He seems to take an instant dislike to Lennie.

Curley's aggressive for no reason. George warns that Curley shouldn't mess with Lennie — this is Steinbeck warning us again about the danger of Lennie, like he does with the mouse in chapter 1.

Lennie's just a big kid — more damn goats...

Lennie's surname is "Small" — what a hilarious joke... hmmmm. Maybe not. Anyway, makes me think of Little John in Robin Hood. It's kind of tragic and almost comical. In fact, it's so funny I think I'm going to bite my face off. Oh yes, there it goes... down to the floor... oh dear.

Chapter Two — Arrival and Introductions

The Ranch hands are pretty *Friendly*

Three of the ranch hands seem much <u>more friendly</u> — Candy, Slim and Carlson.
They're not uptight or on edge, like the boss and Curley seem to be.

1) Candy is <u>helpful</u>, telling them about everyone else.
2) Slim is also <u>friendly</u> and <u>interested</u> in the new arrivals.
3) Carlson is <u>pleasant</u>, but <u>doesn't</u> go out of his way to be friendly.

Candy is <u>definitely</u> the friendliest and most open. He's helpful — though George is <u>wary</u> of him.
He's an experienced ranch-hand, and like his dog, he's seen it all and just wants a <u>quiet life</u>.
But also, he's <u>ancient</u> and close to his sell-by-date. But he doesn't seem to be very bitter.

Curley's "Purty" Wife turns up and Annoys Everyone

She pops into the bunkhouse — twice. She gets a reaction from <u>everyone</u>.

1) She makes George and Candy <u>jumpy</u>.
2) She leans against the doorpost, then tilts and <u>sways her hips</u> forward.
   This leaves Lennie <u>open-mouthed</u>. He says she's "<u>purty</u>".
3) Slim just smiles and <u>flirts</u> mildly with her — "Hi, Good-lookin'".

I can't believe it — my wife's a god damn tramp...

George is probably thinking, "what the hell is going on here?" — and so are we...

All of this makes George *Restless*

George is <u>anxious</u> about the place they've come to.
1) He's <u>suspicious</u> of Candy's warm welcome.
2) He is <u>defensive</u> with the boss's questioning (and rightly so, considering their trouble in Weed).
3) He <u>doesn't like</u> Curley's <u>aggressive attitude</u>, and was <u>disgusted</u> by his gloved hand (see page 22).
4) And he doesn't like Curley's wife either — thinks she's a "<u>tramp</u>", "<u>jail bait</u>", and a "<u>rat-trap</u>".

George is restless because he's worried Lennie will muck things up <u>again</u>:
1) He <u>shouts</u> at him for talking to the boss.
2) He <u>shakes</u> him by his ear when he says Curley's wife is "purty".
3) George is scared he'll "tangle" with Curley himself — because Curley will be looking for a fight with Lennie.

Both Lennie and George are aware that the ranch is <u>dangerous</u>, and <u>neither</u> of them like it.
Steinbeck wants you to feel this sense of fear too — <u>something bad's going to happen</u>.

But it's *Not All Bad*

1) They're about to have lunch <u>without</u> having had to do any work for it.
2) The day after next is Sunday and so it's a day off.
3) There's puppies going spare and Lennie might get one — whoopee!
4) Any money they earn gets the two of them closer to <u>the dream</u>.

Dreams can come true — just not in a Steinbeck novel...

And not in that absolutely awful old Gabrielle song either — I hate that. More than my face.
Steinbeck really structured this section — it's just a load of introductions one after the other.
It's obviously important though, or how else would you know who anyone was, etc...

Chapter Three — It's a Dog's Life

Things begin to turn <u>sour</u> in this section. Curley attacks Lennie, who ends up crushing Curley's hand. Mixed in with this are the dreams of some of the characters — their hopes for future happiness.

> 1) George talks to Slim about Lennie touching the woman's dress in Weed, and them being <u>on the run</u>.
> 2) Candy's dog is executed by Carlson (see page 28 for more).
> 3) Candy joins Lennie and George in the <u>dream</u> of some land.
> 4) Curley's hand is <u>crushed</u> after a fight with Lennie.
> 5) He's then taken to a doctor in town — after Slim forces him to say he got his hand caught in a machine.

...and they say he refused the blindfold.

What a hero. I'm gonna miss that dog *sniff*.

Slim is Nice and Easy-going and George Opens Up to him

George <u>relaxes</u> and chats to Slim. We learn a lot. George really <u>opens up</u> and reveals:

1) He's looked after Lennie since the death of Lennie's Aunt Clara.
2) In the past George has <u>abused his power</u> over Lennie. Once he got Lennie to jump into a river just so he could show off to his friends.
3) George tells how Lennie gets into trouble because he's so "dumb". In Weed he grabbed a woman's dress and wouldn't let go. She claimed he'd <u>raped</u> her and so now they're on the run.
4) Lennie is just a "<u>kid</u>" who's <u>too strong</u> — now he's in danger of killing his new pup through "petting".

Slim's the top man among the men. Everyone has a lot of <u>respect</u> for him. He turns his friendly eyes on the newcomers. He sees that Lennie's not "mean" — not "nasty". He calls George "smart". Though George says that if he was really bright, he'd have his own farm.

Whit is a source of Information and Advice

Whether 'tis nobler in the mind to suffer the slings... oh nuts to this I fancy a biscuit.

Whit likes to <u>bond</u> with others:

1) He plays cards with George, so he can <u>talk</u> to him.
2) He remembers Bill Tenner (a ranch hand he worked with) with <u>affection</u>.
3) He runs out with Carlson to see a <u>possible fight</u> between Slim and Curley.

Whit's also the <u>expert</u> on the Big Saturday Night Out. Susy's is the <u>best brothel</u> to go to, not Clara's. He goes into a fair amount of detail about why it's better (more comfortable chairs, cheaper whisky, and cleaner women). This is what matters to a typical ranch hand.

Carlson is Not so Easy-going

He's a <u>complainer</u> and always sniffing out trouble.
He <u>complains</u> about the <u>smell</u> of Candy's dog — and then kills it. He also:

Carlson, and everyone else, is racist. See page 23 for stuff about racism in the book.

1) <u>complains</u> about the light in the bunkhouse.
2) <u>complains</u> about the "nigger", Crooks — because he always wins the horseshoe game.
3) <u>turns on</u> Curley — "You God damn punk"...."I'll kick your God damn head off".

What's your dog's name — mine won't tell me...

Honestly, he won't. I keep asking him but he just starts to wag his tail. But everyone else knows their dog's name because I can hear them when they're in the park and everywhere. I'm going to ask Rolf Harris I think. He knows about animals. And he could paint me a funny picture too.

Chapter Three — It's a Dog's Life

Carlson kills Candy's dog

Carlson pesters Candy to let him shoot his dog. No one does anything about this.
It's a really grim moment. There's lots more about it on page 28.

There's a chance Dreams could become Reality

Candy overhears George and Lennie's plans for a place of their own. It's such a
wonderful dream that he gets seduced by it too. He wants to join them, and offers:

1)   his compensation money from when he lost his hand.
2)   to make a will handing over his share to them.

George says he has a little farm lined up. They all three decide to buy it at the end of the month,
when George and Lennie have $50 each from their work.

This is probably the happiest and most optimistic bit of the whole book. You start to believe their
dream is possible. You know it's a great idea and forget it's a dream — it seems to be changing
into a practical plan. And George himself — perhaps for the one and only time — seems to believe
and enjoy it. He's not just saying things to keep his mate Lennie happy. He sees a way out.

Curly and Lennie's Fight Shatters the Dream

This chapter just gets worse — after Candy's dog is killed, Curley attacks Lennie.

1)   Slim bursts in and Curley follows, grovelling — he's just accused Slim of messing with his wife.
2)   Carlson starts hassling Curley, stirring up trouble — "you're as yella as a frog".
3)   Even one-handed Candy joins in the argument — "'Glove fulla Vaseline'", he yells in disgust.
4)   Curley is cornered — but spots Lennie smiling (still about the dream).
5)   Curley orders Lennie to his feet and starts punching him in the face.
6)   Lennie is scared and doesn't fight back — he calls to George for help.

Have a look at page 20 to see what this is about.

This carries on until George orders Lennie to "Get 'im".

1)   It's like the mice and the Weed girl and his brown and white pup — once Lennie has hold of
something he's slow to let go. He's grabbed Curley's hand and now won't let go.
2)   Curley's hand is crushed.
3)   Slim pressurises Curley to say he crushed it in a machine, so he won't get Lennie fired.
4)   Curley is taken off to the doctor's.

The Atmosphere is Grim

Oh dear. Lennie and George's jobs may be safe for now. But things feel grim:

1)   There's a lot of tension and conflict around the ranch.
2)   Lennie's physical strength has again destroyed something unintentionally.
3)   It could easily happen again.

Ever since I left Susy's somethin' ain't been right...

What should have been a quiet Friday night — looking forward to the big
Saturday night out — ends in disaster. Curley has just one hand left.

Tension and conflict — typical Friday night if you ask me...

Lennie wouldn't fight until George told him to. Slim was ready to jump in but George stopped him —
he ordered Lennie to "Get 'im". And at the end Lennie cries, "I didn't wanta". So maybe Lennie isn't
mean, but is just like a big kid (doing what he was told...). Or a raving nutcase who likes to stroke.

Chapter Four — Curley's Wife Spoils Things

After the last chapter things take a bit of a turn for the better in this one... the lowest of the lows on the ranch (that's Crooks, Candy and Lennie) all dreaming of a way out. Ahh... hang on a bit... Ah, I forgot about the end of the chapter. It's really depressing. All the dreams fade away... Doh.

1) This chapter takes place in Crooks' room. Candy, Lennie and Crooks meet.
2) In the social life of the ranch, they're the lowest ranking characters.
3) It's now Saturday night and all the other men are visiting a brothel in town.
4) Crooks is wary of the others at first but he slowly gets friendlier.
5) After talking they realise they have dreams in common.
6) Curley's wife comes in and shatters the dream and breaks up the party.

Lennie and then Candy visit Crooks

This chapter is set in Crooks' room — it's feels different because:

1) It's actually both his workshop and his home.
2) It's completely separate from the bunkhouse — he's kept apart from the whites. He's the only black worker.

The chapter starts with Crooks rubbing liniment into his back (to ease the pain). Then:

1) Lennie comes in, smiling stupidly. Crooks tells him to get out.
2) But Lennie's smile wins him over — it's innocent and "disarming".
3) Crooks teases him about George never coming back. He pushes him as far as he can until Lennie gets "quiet and mad". Crooks realises he isn't malicious or nasty. He won't "blab".
4) Lennie starts talking about The Dream, and his stupid optimism about it wins Crooks over.
5) Candy comes in. He's already dreaming of his part on George and Lennie's little farm.
6) Crooks is won over by The Dream too — he lived on a similar farm when he was a boy. He wants to join in the plan, and offers to work for nothing.

This is about as optimistic (although in a very naive way) as the book gets. All three characters are right at the bottom of the heap — but they're full of hope and can all see a way out.

Lennie, Candy and Crooks get Dreaming

It's pretty well the midpoint of the story and these three blokes are on a high. For a few blissful moments these three are companions, future business partners and fellow dreamers:

1) Lennie dreams of living off the "fatta the lan'" and being chief rabbit-keeper.
2) Candy has an idea for making money out of the rabbits.
3) Crooks promises to work "Like a son-of-a-bitch" for nothing.

You're reading this and you think — "Yes, this is possible." These men could — just possibly — create this heaven on earth. Here are some men actually getting on well together and properly relating to each other. It's a special but all-too-brief moment in the whole book.

But then again, it really doesn't seem all that likely — they're just dreaming and talking, and none of them have any real power, and you don't really believe that it's going to happen.

The optimism and hope in this briefly shared dream is shattered by Curley's wife — there's a big contrast between her coarseness and the ideal, childlike image of the dream.

Chapter Four — Curley's Wife Spoils Things

Curley's Wife Breaks up the Party

Just when everyone was getting along fine, Curley's wife comes from out of nowhere. Her entrance is a shock to the three blokes. Steinbeck emphasises this by not giving her an introduction — she just starts talking, with her catchphrase of course... "Any you boys seen Curley?".

Curley's wife doesn't like these three men. They're the "weak ones". She thinks that:

1) Crooks is just a "nigger",
2) Lennie is a "dum-dum" and,
3) Candy is a "lousy old sheep".

Curley's wife thinks she knows all about men — all of them

Like Crooks she's on the defensive at first. She says she can get along fine with men individually (probably by flirting), but not with a group of men. She finds men defensive and competitive. Curley's wife believes she knows all about men:

1) She says she hates them and knows all about their weakness for drink.
2) She seems to like putting them down. It probably makes her feel better.
3) She's even happy that big Lennie "bust up Curley".
4) She threatens Crooks — "I could get you strung up on a tree so easy it ain't even funny".
     She's hinting that she could claim he raped her, and he'd be found guilty because he's black.

This scene is all about Power

This is all about power. She gets comfort from the feeling of being superior to these men. She ends up breaking the bonds between these three new chums. It's another pessimistic view of women in this book. (see page 33 for more about the Battle of the Sexes)

When the Men Return from Town it's Back to Reality

It's all back to normal when the men get back — blacks and whites are separated, and the dreams that just a few minutes ago were almost possible are now again impossible.

1) Curley's wife slips out when she hears the other men get back.
2) Crooks tells the others to leave him.
3) Lennie gets told off by George for being there.

As for the dream, Crooks says he no longer wants to work on the shared farm:
"I didn't mea' it" ... "Just foolin'" — he says.

It seems they're all doomed to work hard for someone else, so someone else can get rich.
Crooks once again puts "liniment" onto his aching back.
This is reality — it's returned to a focus on pain and work.
It's a really depressing end to the chapter, especially because things just a moment ago were looking good, just for a while. There was some hope.

Where's my dream — where is it? I can't go on like this...

No one likes having their dreams destroyed. I remember when I was thirteen and I really liked this girl. I mean, really liked her. Though she barely knew I existed. Stephanie, she was called. Then one day she walked into school and said she was moving to Bristol. All my dreams were shattered... sob...

Chapter Five — A Dead Girl and a Dead Dream

This is the section where Lennie kills Curley's wife. Then he has to be hunted down.
It all happens on the Sunday — the day of rest. A peaceful Sunday afternoon — ironic, eh...

1) Lennie's in the barn with a dead puppy — he's just killed it.
2) Curley's wife enters and talks about her past and her dreams of the stage.
3) She asks Lennie to feel her soft hair — he does and he likes it.
4) She tries to pull away, but he holds on. She tries to scream, but he puts his hand over her mouth and shakes her. He breaks her neck. She's dead. Lennie runs away.
5) Candy finds her dead and gets George, who plans to kill Lennie himself.
6) The other guys come in, and decide to go after Lennie and kill him.

In the Barn

Lennie has killed his pup:

1) One moment he was caressing his pup, the next it's dead.
2) He's angry with it because he's now terrified George won't let him tend the rabbits.

This is the glum and angry mood Curley's wife finds him in. It's the first time they're together alone.

Here Comes Trouble

Curley's wife comes across Lennie and does the thing she knows best — flirts. OR she might actually be lonely — it's difficult to tell. She doesn't know how else to communicate with men. Maybe Steinbeck is showing how society has forced people into stereotyped roles. Who knows...

Anyway, this is what she does, in her "Curley's wife" way...

1) She soothes and comforts him.
2) She expresses her bitterness with her life in general and with men in particular.
3) She continues to dream — "Maybe I will yet". She isn't used to living like this. She still hopes to make something of herself.

Curley's wife starts to talk about herself, and to confide in Lennie. We learn that:

1) She only married Curley on the rebound. Her dreams of pictures and shows hadn't happened.
2) She hates being lonely. She chose Curley probably to get away from her mother. He's the third best after the films and the stage.

Both she and Lennie are obsessed with themselves and their own hopes.
At this moment, each feels under threat.

Lennie Strokes Her Hair, She Screams and then She's Dead

Most of the time during their conversation, Lennie and Curley's wife are not really communicating. They just ramble on about their own problems without listening — it's not a proper conversation. Then they find they have something in common — they both like soft things: hair, velvet, fur, silk.

Lennie now does the same thing as he did to the mice, the woman in Weed, and his own little pup.

1) He switches suddenly from being gentle to being violent.
2) One moment he's ecstatically stroking her hair, the next he's breaking her neck.
3) But it's because he's afraid, like an animal. And most animals won't harm you if you leave them alone.

Curley's wife goes limp "like a fish". It's an awful image in a horrific and pathetic scene.
What he did to Curley's hand, he's now done to Curley's wife.

Chapter Five — A Dead Girl and a Dead Dream

Now Everyone's Dreams are Over

In the latest fit of panic from Lennie, you could say all these characters have lost their dreams:

George

George now knows he'll end up spending his monthly wages on women and whisky — "I think I knowed we'd never do her." He wears a "black hat" — like an executioner.

Lennie

Lennie remembers the back-up plan to go to the place down by the river. So he does.

Candy

One last time Candy imagines the little farm that would have been their own. It could have been perfect — a happy mix of work and leisure. Then he breaks down in tears. He says Lennie was "such a nice fella", and Curley's wife was a "poor bastard".

Curley's Wife

She is still beautiful — even when she's dead, lying in the hay. Her dreams of getting into the pictures or onto the stage are also now dead.

All Curley wants is Revenge — for his Wife AND His Hand

Curley has not only lost his wife — he's been humiliated... twice. He's a hard-hearted man:

1) He doesn't touch his wife (Slim does that).
2) And he doesn't stay with her (as Slim suggests).

Curley is a cold man — he just wants Lennie dead.

> I'm gonna horseshoe him to death.

Slim touches Curley's Wife

It's Slim, not Curley, who goes over to Curley's wife. We are told Slim:

1) went over "quietly", not efficiently, and he "felt her wrist" rather than taking her pulse.
2) "touched her cheek" and "explored" her neck.

This moment is very tender and the others hang back — there could be a lot of reasons why Steinbeck described it this way. Here are a few to think about (or learn...).

1) It shows Slim's authority and his position as the humane 'spiritual' leader of the men.
2) It emphasises the impact of Lennie's actions and remind us that a real person is dead.
3) It suggests a personal response from Slim, perhaps implying he did feel affection for her.

Whatever — one thing is clear: Slim is moved somehow, and Curley's just being a fool...

George plans to Kill Lennie

> Of course Steinbeck doesn't tell you at the time — that would just ruin the ending.

George knows he has to get to Lennie before Curley and the rest do. He has to save Lennie from Curley. But he has to cover his tracks too, so:

1) he gets Candy to pretend to discover the body. So they won't think he's in on it, he says.
2) he rejects the idea of letting Lennie run free — he'll starve.
3) he comes up with the idea of saving Lennie by killing him himself.

Drop the dead dream — or the goat gets it...

Only when Curley's wife is dead is she beautiful and innocent. And only then does she get attention from the men — and that was her dream. It's like Steinbeck's saying "You have to die for dreams to come true". Which isn't too cheery. Think I might go and cry. Over Stephanie still...

Chapter Six — George Kills his Best Friend

Notice how the story ends where it begins. It's come full circle. Lennie and then George return to the riverbank where it all started a couple of days ago.

1) Lennie's at the pool. He 'sees' Aunt Clara who lectures him, and a rabbit, who mocks him.
2) George arrives. He recites The Dream to Lennie. And then shoots him in the back of the head.
3) The other men turn up. Slim realises what George has done and comforts him.
4) The book ends with Carlson saying "Now what the hell ya suppose is eatin' them two guys?".

Lennie Dies in a Place of Death and Destiny

It couldn't have happened in a more beautiful spot.

It's dusk — it's a turning point, and everything is on the move:

1) The light is fading by the minute.
2) The wind picks up, and then dies down.
3) A heron takes off.

> Lennie has a dream of going away and living in a cave, like an animal. When he returns to the pool, in nature, you sense it's where he belongs — he is an animal, and doesn't fit into the human world.

It's a Place of Death because:

1) A heron gobbles up a watersnake.
2) Lennie has previously killed mice here.
3) Lennie is about to be killed here.

It's a Place of Destiny because:

1) They'd always arranged to meet here in case of trouble. George had sensed it was going to be needed.
2) One of the very last things Lennie does is unwittingly saves the life of a watersnake by disturbing a heron.

He Feels Guilty — He Remembers Being Told Off in the Past

Lennie knows he's done a "bad thing". Because of this two visions come out of his head. Both speak in his voice. He's heard these lectures so often, he's saying them to himself.

The key things are:

1) Aunt Clara is very much an authority figure for him, and also maternal (like a mother).
2) She says George is a "nice fella", and goes on about how he was always good to Lennie.
3) She accuses Lennie of never taking any care and of doing a "bad thing". He has let George down.

This is the guilt coming out, gnawing away at him.

The Giant Rabbit Threatens that Lennie will Never Change

1) The rabbit accuses him of what he'll do in the future — he'll forget to tend his rabbits.
2) It says George probably won't let him look after the rabbits anyway.
3) It says George will beat him with a stick.
4) And then George will desert him.

Only the third one comes true (sort of) — but George doesn't beat Lennie with a stick — he kills him with a gun.

LENNIE SMALL!!! I'm a gonna pull your head off!!!

Uh-oh...

Lennie's deepest fears (his hurt, anger and despair) come out in these visions. His dream was to look after rabbits — and it's a rabbit that is mocking him. This shows that on some level he knows his dream can't come true.

Chapter Six — George Kills his Best Friend

George <u>Saves</u> Lennie By <u>Killing Him</u>

At the moment of Lennie's <u>greatest need</u>, with the rabbit tormenting him, George arrives.
Three options are discussed now. Three dreams of the <u>future</u> *(though 1 and 2 are kind of the same thing).*

1) George could live <u>on his own</u> and blow his money every
    month on <u>women and whisky</u>.
2) Lennie suggests he go off and <u>live in a cave by himself</u>.
3) George and Lennie could live off the "fatta the lan'".

Most dreams in this novel are a form of <u>Self-Deception</u>

And George now <u>deliberately deceives</u> Lennie.

> The final recital of their dream is used to prepare Lennie for his <u>execution</u>.
> Lennie is <u>so excited</u>, so wound up in feverish anticipation, he keeps prompting George.
> He says more about their dream this time than he ever has <u>before</u>.
> Lennie's <u>happiness and childlike</u> hope makes the whole execution thing <u>much much worse</u>.

Lennie has run out of patience. He wants his dream <u>now</u> — "Le's get that place now."
But while for Lennie "that place" is the little farm, the reality is — "that place" is <u>death</u>.

Lennie has been <u>destroyed</u> by the <u>words of Aunt Clara</u> and the <u>rabbit</u>, and the <u>bullet in the head</u>.

> **LENNIE IS SHOT LIKE AN ANIMAL**
> The bunkhouse guys <u>no longer</u> want Lennie alive — just like
> with Candy's poor old dog. Again Lennie is like an <u>animal</u>.
> He's shot <u>like Candy's dog</u> — in the back of the head.

The Characters <u>React Differently</u> to the Death

George

Tells everyone he <u>took the gun off Lennie</u>.
They all think Lennie <u>stole it</u> from Carlson.

Curley

He's always kidded himself he was a <u>great fighter</u>.
He now kids himself it was his bullet which took
Lennie out. <u>Pompous prat</u>.

Slim

He knows <u>straight away</u> what has really happened. Slim is "<u>Godlike</u>" — he knows and sees <u>everything</u>.
But he doesn't say anything about it and he <u>comforts George</u>.

Carlson

Carlson's a <u>cold man</u>. He <u>can't understand</u> what George and Slim have got to be so <u>thoughtful</u> about.
"Now what the hell ya suppose is eatin' them two guys?" he says to Curley. Carlson has <u>no dreams</u>.
He <u>fits in</u> with ranch life and accepts its <u>cruelty</u>.

Saw a giant rabbit once — it told me to burn things...

And so I did I burned all my toys and my little sister's favourite doll ~~Ben loved~~ till her face was melted
and then my mum said I could only ~~get~~ ~~destroy for a month~~ as punishment but my skin went purple
and I had to ~~go to hospital~~ and I could hear the nurses laughing at my purple face and purple pee.

NO, NO, NO! THIS IS NOT RELEVANT!

Revision Summary

We've reached that time — that oh so glorious time — where you have to actually try and remember what you've been reading about so far. This is definitely the least enjoyable bit of studying — no wait. I'm so sorry. That made it sound like studying is actually really fun for the rest of the time. How foolish of me. I apologise. In any case, you still have to answer the questions below. Look some of them up at first if you have to, but you should end up knowing all the answers off the top of your head.

Chapter One

1) Which of these words best describes George's reactions to Lennie: a) harassed b) comforting c) apologetic or d) all of these?

2) Do you think George would be happy without Lennie (based on what he says in chapter one)? Write a paragraph explaining your answer.

3) Do you think it's significant that they eat beans with no ketchup? Why?

4) Does this first chapter make you interested in what happens to Lennie and George in the rest of the book? Explain why.

Chapter Two

5) Do you think the boss is a nice guy? Give three reasons.

6) Why do you think Curley takes an instant dislike to Lennie?

7) Write a sentence that sums up the way Slim is described when he first appears in this chapter.

8) Write a paragraph saying whether you think Lennie likes the ranch or not.

Chapter Three

9) Why did George and Lennie have to get out of Weed?

10) Why do you think Carlson wants to kill Candy's dog?

11) Do you think that George and Lennie's dream could come true (based only on the section in chapter three where they discuss it with Candy)?

12) Whose fault is it that Lennie ends up crushing Curley's hand? Explain your answer fully.

Chapter Four

13) Do you think Crooks likes having Lennie in his room?

14) Do you think Curley's wife is racist? Back up your argument with at least three points, and explain each one fully.

15) As they're leaving Crooks' room, Crooks tells Candy that he doesn't want to be any part of their dream after all. Why do you think Crooks says this?

Chapter Five

16) Do you think Curley's wife is flirting with Lennie in this section? Why?

17) Why do you think Lennie kills Curley's wife?

18) Which of these best sums up Curley's reaction to the death of his wife? a) broken hearted b) emotionally distraught c) pretty happy d) hungry for revenge or e) thirsty for soda pop.

Chapter Six

19) What do you think Lennie's hallucinations are meant to show the reader?

20) Would you be scared of a six foot rabbit?

21) Choose the word that you think describes Lennie's death most accurately, and explain why in detail: a) execution b) murder c) destiny

Now what the hell ya suppose is eatin' them two guys

George (part 1)

Slim says not many do what George does — team up with a friend to work on the ranches. You've got to admire him for looking after Lennie. But he pays for it in the end — he has to kill his friend.

George has No Problems when he's On His Own

1) George is <u>reasonably smart</u>. He's clever as far as finding work is concerned.
2) He's "<u>small</u>" and "<u>quick</u>", "dark of face, with restless eyes, and sharp, strong features".
   He has "small strong hands", "slender arms", and a "thin and bony nose".
3) He's got <u>no family</u>, no land, no wife and no money.
4) He tends to be <u>suspicious</u> of people when he first meets them — often on the defensive.
5) He's often <u>pessimistic</u>. "It don't make no difference" he says at the very end. This is typical of him.

He regularly says he'd be better off <u>on his own</u>. He's tempted to ditch Lennie, but his feelings of <u>responsibility</u> towards Lennie are greater than the temptation. For example, he <u>saved Lennie's life</u> in Weed. They had to hide in an irrigation ditch all day. It was pretty desperate stuff.

George is Trapped in his partnership with Lennie

1) His <u>conscience</u> and sense of <u>loyalty</u> mean he sticks by Lennie.
2) He's Lennie's minder and instructor — always telling him what to do and how to behave — probably always wondering what Lennie's up to (Lennie hides stuff from him like a little kid).
3) He's <u>nervous</u> that Lennie could get into trouble at any time and make things difficult for them <u>both</u>. So at the pool he tells Lennie to <u>say nothing</u> when they meet the boss. And he tells him to be <u>wary</u> of Curley and to meet back at the "brush" if anything goes badly wrong.
4) He's often irritated because of the trouble he has looking after Lennie.
5) Since saving him from drowning in a river — after <u>telling him</u> to jump in — he wants to do what's best for Lennie. He says he now <u>regrets</u> having abused his power.

George knows Lennie and all his little (weirdy) ways. It's <u>like a marriage</u> — they've been through so much together and it seems they'll <u>always be together</u>.

George is mostly...		
Bitter	Worried	Serious
Annoyed	Weary	Small

George has pretty bad Mood Swings

1) Sometimes George is <u>optimistic</u>, sometimes grimly <u>pessimistic</u>, and with Lennie at times <u>aggressive</u> and at others gentle and <u>reassuring</u>.
2) He's <u>unhappy</u> at the start. They have <u>fled Weed</u> because of Lennie stroking a girl's red dress. The bus driver dropped them some way from the ranch. And Lennie is asking too many questions.
3) But when he settles down that first night under the stars, he <u>seems happy</u>. It seems a perfect spot. He can stare up into the night sky. There are no bosses here. And perhaps he can sleep and <u>dream</u>.
4) But he's <u>usually irritable</u> with Lennie. You get the impression he's had years of stress and worry over him.
5) And he <u>regrets</u> not having his own <u>girlfriend</u> — Lennie gets in the way.
6) He's <u>negative</u> about the new job, but does cheer up a bit after Candy has talked to him for a while.

George is moody. But this is understandable — he's got this <u>complicated commitment</u> to Lennie. And life could go either way... the farm of his dreams or a life of work for a few measly dollars.

George (part 2)

George is a pretty Aggressive bloke

1) He hates Curley immediately, because he's aggressive towards them (especially to Lennie) straight away. Also, Curley has things George doesn't. And he hasn't earned them. He has a permanent position on the farm because of who his father is. And he's got a beautiful wife. He tells Lennie to "let 'im have it" if Curley hits him, and says, "I'm scared I'm gonna tangle with that bastard myself."

2) He doesn't seem to like Curley's wife — "I seen 'em poison before." He thinks women 'like her' are dangerous. (He's sort of proved right later.)

3) He still shouts at Lennie a lot (and he used to bully him).

4) When Candy tries to muscle in on their dream, George is immediately defensive: "you got nothing to do with us".

5) He generally hates his life. He doesn't even have control of his own food — fed by a "lap cook" (on the ranch). It's like having to live on school dinners all the time. Imagine the horror...

He has No Control of His Life

This life on the road, moving from job to job has clearly taken its toll. George is very cynical about anything going his way. He has no control over his life:

1) He has to obey others all the time.
2) He's tied to Lennie and tied to the need to work.
3) He has to take orders from people he doesn't respect.
4) People give him a hard time — even the bus driver drops them several miles away from the ranch.

George is weary of all this — he wants to escape... to the dream of a farm.

His dreams Keep Him Going

Sometimes he recites the dream of land and rabbits just to keep Lennie happy (like in Chapter One). But occasionally he gets so sucked in, he believes it himself — like when he's talking about it with Lennie and Candy in Chapter Three.

However, he is hopeful about Candy's offer of money. He sees it is practical. And it's something that can happen now. This is good because they're not in a great place — with Curley and his wife looking likely to be trouble hotspots.

The way George looks at the sky in Chapter One, it's as if he'd really like to be up there. Maybe the sky represents freedom from all the hassles of looking after Lennie, and the daily grind of work.

But in the end, he says it "don't make no difference". He actually reassures Lennie that he hasn't "done another bad thing". But you could say George now thinks that whatever you do in life makes no difference — nothing matters. Lennie is killed and with it dies George's reason for believing he could live independently, on "the fat of the lan'", on a farm of their own.

Georgie, George, tell me a story (about rabbits)...

At first George seems really normal. But I think he's actually just a weirdo like the rest of them. He wanders around the country with some bloke doing work he hates, getting bitterer and bitterer.

Lennie (part 1)

Lennie is the <u>central character</u>. He's perhaps the most <u>interesting</u> character in the novel. He's likeable and even loveable — maybe because he himself is so keen to show affection. We also know that there's a huge part of him that means no harm. But he's <u>not harmless</u>. He's both <u>villain and victim</u>, and <u>caring and destructive</u>. He's <u>complicated</u> — even <u>contradictory</u>.

He's a huge, grown man — but also very *Childlike*

1) He's a <u>powerful man with huge hands</u> — a brilliant farm labourer.
2) He may have grown up physically but he <u>hasn't grown up mentally</u> — Slim says "he's jes like a kid". And Slim should know. He's a bright bloke.
3) Lennie's <u>innocent</u> — he doesn't know how to behave. He also asks lots of innocent questions. Slim says he can see immediately that Lennie "aint mean".
4) He <u>isn't very interested</u> in other people — apart from beautiful women.
5) He <u>takes orders</u> from George. And he can also take orders from Slim about "petting" his new puppy. This is important. It is clear that Lennie doesn't want to disobey ANYONE or do anything wrong.

So — he takes orders and can slave away, like a machine. In other words, he's a very useful person for George to have teamed up with, because he'll earn <u>loads of cash</u>.

Curley's wife calls him a "<u>dum-dum</u>". Earlier, Slim says he seems a bit of a "<u>cuckoo</u>" — "<u>crazy</u>". But George quickly <u>denies it</u> — Lennie is "dumb as hell" certainly but he's not insane. But when we see what Lennie <u>does</u> during the course of the book, you wonder... He's subject to <u>violent fits</u> and may be mentally ill, but we don't know — these things weren't properly diagnosed back then.

Lennie is mostly...	Big	Violent	Childish
	Stupid	Strong	Like an animal

He *Identifies with Animals*

1) He looks <u>like a bear</u>, and walks like one — "he walked heavily, dragging his feet a little, the way a bear drags his paws". He also eats and drinks like a <u>hungry animal</u>.
2) He slavers and <u>drools over beautiful women</u> (e.g. Curley's wife). He can't control some of his animal instincts, it seems.
3) Right from childhood he has befriended animals before people — and it has to be *cuddly* animals. His Aunt Clara used to give him mice to play with.
4) He's stubborn and <u>very possessive</u> over his animals (e.g. over his pet mice, pup and his dream of tending his own rabbits). He never wants to let the animals we see him with out of his sight. But he's not very good at deceiving George — he knows whenever Lennie's got one hidden in his coat or in his pocket.
5) Lennie's always on the lookout for a pet — a mouse, a rabbit or a pup (or maybe a "<u>purty</u>" woman).

He loves tame and friendly animals — that's mostly what he is himself... <u>tame and friendly</u>. The mother of his new brown and white pup allows him to handle all the others — "...she don't care. She lets me." Animals seem unusually <u>comfortable and unthreatened</u> by him.

<u>BUT...</u> there's another side to this obsession with animals. He's also got a male animal's <u>sex drive</u>. This expresses itself in his desire to stroke soft things — the lady in Weed's dress and Curley's wife's hair, for example. This seems <u>sexual</u>, but Lennie's not mature enough to understand it. In both cases, whatever the motivation behind it, the consequences were very bad.

Lennie (part 2)

He's dependent on George in both Body and Mind

1) George has adopted his friend, Lennie, after Lennie's Aunt Clara's death.
2) Lennie couldn't survive on his own. He has none of the independence or practical skills of most adults. He wouldn't be able to sort out food and shelter for himself. This is despite his repeated offer of going off on his own and living in a cave. He may in some ways be animal-like but he probably wouldn't survive a week out in the wild.
3) George is the only person who stimulates his mind, filling it with the dream of owning and farming their own land. Lennie is, in a way, addicted to this vision — pleading with George to tell him about it whenever he gets the chance.
4) He gets himself into scrapes and he needs George to get him out of them — like with Curley. He'd probably have been lynched (punished or hanged without a trial) or locked up ages ago if George hadn't stepped in.

So George is both his parent and big brother, his guardian and friend. He's always there for him. George knows Lennie inside out. Lennie can't keep secrets from him (like hiding mice in his pockets).

Perhaps this isn't surprising:

1) Lennie has been with him for a long time.
2) And has been dependent on him all that time.

Lennie does however give something in return — he's a good worker (does the work of two men). This is very useful for George. It helps them get and keep work (until Lennie mucks it all up).

George is, in a way, Lennie's manager — and one who now does the best for him.

But Lennie's also a Killer

This is one of the key things in the whole novel. The gentlest man is also the most destructive. He's dangerous, and a violent killer:

1) He attacks Curley, Curley's wife, kills mice and throws his dead pup onto the barn floor in anger.
2) But it's not malicious (mean). He doesn't want to cause pain — e.g. when he fights Curley he's actually encouraged by George: "Get 'im, Lennie!" Lennie says afterwards he "didn't wanta hurt him."

There are two sides to the story here:

1) Lennie has little self-restraint. Everything he does is in extremes.
2) He's liable to panic when someone else does (e.g. with Curley's wife). In these panic attacks things tend to happen too suddenly — one minute he's stroking Curley's wife's hair the next he's broken her neck. And even George can't get him to stop crushing Curley's hand.

This is the tragedy of Lennie's life — friendliness turns into aggression.
As George says, he "don't know no rules".
But Lennie's aggression is innocent — that's what makes it different from the others'.

Lennie's a big weirdo with a nasty stroking fetish...

Or is he? I mean, I always stroke dogs when they come up to me, and I don't think that's sexual. People stroke pet cats and dogs all the time. Maybe we're all twisted. Apart from me, naturally...

Carlson

You've probably read the book and thought that Carlson is just another ranch hand — he doesn't do much and he doesn't say much. Well... I'm afraid, Mr. Bond, that you are very much mistaken.

> Carlson makes things happen. He takes an _active part_ in key events:
> 1)   He shoots Candy's dog.
> 2)   He turns on Curley, which leads to Lennie crushing his hand.
> 3)   His gun is used to kill Lennie.
> 4)   He has the last word in the book.

Carlson is a bit of a Stirrer...

Carlson seems to enjoy conflict. He even stirs things up to get it. When Curley is apologising to Slim for asking him too often where his wife is, Carlson jumps in. He:

1)   tells Curley to tell his wife to stay at home,
2)   tells him he's a coward — "yella as a frog belly",
3)   calls him a "God damn punk",
4)   gloats over the fact Curley has had to grovel,
5)   threatens Curley — "You come for me, an' I'll kick your God damn head off."

> He doesn't actually get involved in the fights though — maybe he's all talk...

Carlson also complains all the time... like about:

1)   the darkness in the bunkhouse,
2)   Crooks always winning the horseshoe game,
3)   the smell of Candy's dog.

> Carlson is mostly...
>
> | | |
> |---|---|
> | Tactless | Complaining |
> | Stupid | Stirring |
> | Big | There |

Carlson is Mr Insensitive

Carlson never thinks about anyone's feelings. When he's tired of Candy's dog being about the place and stinking, he just suggests it should be shot, and that Candy could have a puppy instead.

Carlson's got no tact — like when he's going on about the dog, in front of Candy and everyone:

1)   He points at the dog with his boot to show where he's going to shoot it.
2)   After shooting it, he cleans the gun in full view of everyone in the bunkhouse.
3)   There's never any apology — he just says "He won't even feel it."

AND Carlson is not perceptive — he doesn't really know what's going on at the end of the novel:

1)   He doesn't realise George stole his gun to shoot Lennie with.
2)   He can't think why Slim leads George away from the riverbank.
     "...what the hell ya suppose is eating them two guys?"

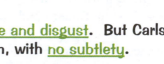

He hasn't worked out what has really happened — whereas Slim has.
This is a novel about hugely complex emotions like hope and despair, love and disgust. But Carlson isn't really plugged into these things. The world is black and white to him, with no subtlety.

Carlson is your stereotypical insensitive cowboy...

Think about those words in the red box when you think of Carlson — he's tactless, stupid, big, complaining and stirring. Don't just dismiss him — say he's important to the book. Really important, with his big stupid moaning and his nasty "shoot the dog" attitude. I'll give him dog...

Curley

Write about Curley referring to relationships, restlessness, and fighting and you'll be fine.

> *Curley* is brought to you by the words...
> | | |
> |---|---|
> | Anxious | Insecure |
> | Restless | Lonely |
> | Aggressive | Angry |

Relationships — No one likes Curley

Let's face it, Curley should have a lot going for him.
He's young, fit and healthy. He's the boss's son.
AND, hey, he's just married an attractive woman. BUT...

1) No one likes him — he gets no respect from anyone.
2) So he must be very lonely.
3) Slim and Carlson threaten him. And they order him to lie about how his hand got crushed.
4) And he has no control over his flirtatious wife — he's picked the wrong wife
   (remember... we only see him with her when she's dead — it's a disastrous marriage).

He may have posh "high-heeled boots". But he's still an anxious little man. A little man who's power mad. A little man who hates big guys. Jealous, clearly. Insecure, clearly. He's a failure. He never gets what he wants. Even right at the end he doesn't get to shoot Lennie.

> **That Glove Full of Vaseline**
>
> *"Keepin' that hand soft for his wife"... it's a nasty thought. You could say he wants to be soft on the inside and hard on the outside — if you want to be clever. Or he might just be weird.*

Restlessness — Curley is Really Jumpy

1) Curley is really restless — Whit says he's got "yella-jackets in his drawers" (ants in his pants).
2) Curley's an outsider — he's not one of the bunkhouse men.
3) He's not even happy in his new marriage. His wife flirts with other men and he never knows where she is.
4) Because he's jumpy he picks fights with the wrong men (like Slim and Lennie) to try and prove something.

He's nervous. Actually, he's more than that — he's neurotic. About everything and everyone. He's always on the move, storming in and out of places — itching for a fight, searching for his wife, looking for his father... in the end, hunting down Lennie. Even when he's standing still he's clenching his fists — he's on edge.

Fighting — Curley's "Always Scrappy"

1) Curley looks like a boxer. A small boxer, that is.
2) Candy says he's "handy". That means he fights well.
   Whit says he was in the finals for the "Golden Gloves" (a boxing competition).
3) Fighting's the one thing he's good at. And we all like to show off at what we're good at.
4) He sizes up George and Lennie immediately, and picks on Lennie because he's big — Candy says he "hates big guys", and is "alla time picking scraps with big guys".
5) He wants an audience. He craves attention and respect, wanting to be admired and accepted.

Curley is a hateful, surly, mean little excuse for a man...

Curley wants to be the big bad boss. But he's not — it's just a dream, like the bunkhouse guys' dreams of some land and a farm. He hates anyone who challenges this dream. But I must say I'm not surprised. Wouldn't you hate a surly little vaseline-rubbing trouble-making fist-fighting swine?

Crooks

Old Crooks may not appear much in the book — but he says some important things. He's suffered and been treated differently because he's black.

Only Crooks has a Room of his Own

1) It's small, basic and functional.
2) But it's homely and it's his own — it's full of his possessions.
3) People who try to come into his room get a frosty reception
   — Lennie, Candy and Curley's wife all find this.
4) He looks after his room. It shows he's "a proud, aloof man",
   whose eyes seem "to glitter with intensity".
5) The fact he has this room of his own shows how separated from the others he is.

> **Crooks is...**
> Cynical   In pain
> Scapegoated   Proud
> Crippled   At the bottom

But when Crooks is actually with the others — like slinging horseshoes — he can be the best.

He's the Only One with many Personal Possessions

The contents of Crook's room tell you what his life's like:

1) He is practical and active — rubber boots, a big alarm clock and a shotgun.
2) His books show that he reads and thinks — a "tattered dictionary"
   and a "mauled copy of the Californian Civil Code for 1905".
3) His tools show he's skilled and very capable with his hands.
4) His medicine shows that like Candy he's getting old and decrepit after a lifetime of work.

Crooks is a Victim of Racism

> **Crooks the Bully**
> Crooks senses that Lennie is below him in the 'natural order' of the ranch. He immediately abuses this power, suggesting that George has left Lennie. He takes "pleasure in his torture". This an example of the bullied becoming the bully.

America was a very racist place in 1937, when this book was published. Crooks' life probably represents the experience of many black men in America then.

1) Crooks is the only black man in the book.
2) He's excluded from and generally not wanted in the bunkhouse.
3) The ranch men say he stinks — but he thinks THEY all stink.
4) He's picked on — he's a scapegoat. Candy tells us the boss "gives him hell when he's mad".
5) He's lonely — he misses the companionship of others — he says this to Lennie.
6) His face is lined with pain and his back is crippled from overwork.

He's a Survivor — but has Little Power in the Ranch

There's no justice. Crooks has skills at work that no one else has (he's best at the horseshoe game) but is at the bottom of the pile —. But this isn't a world where the best get to the top...

1) He was kicked and crippled by a horse years ago.
2) He has been and is racially abused all the time.
3) He's excluded from almost everything.

What's important is who has the power to start with (like Curley's dad being the boss). Crooks certainly wasn't born with, and doesn't have, any power. He tries to stand up to Curley's wife — but fails — she could have him lynched, by saying he tried to rape her.

Another depressing story... whatever next...

Crooks talks "dreamily" of the past — his dad's chicken farm that was lost. He thinks the dreams of others either won't happen or will fail. He's seen too many men "with land in their head" that are just kidding themselves. He knows the reality is that the men spend any savings in the whorehouse.

Whit

Whit's a naive and enthusiastic young ranch hand. Not yet jaded by full-time work... Lucky man.

Whit is a Young man Destined for a Life on the Ranch

Whit's role is as a fun guy — hence his 'funny' name. He's likeable because of:

1) His youth, innocence and friendliness.
2) His helpful knowledge of working life on the farm.
3) His attitude — he's not bitter about being trapped in ranch life.
   He could turn into a sad old figure like Candy. But he isn't aware of it.

He's Open, Friendly and keen to Impress

Whit's the young face on the ranch — enthusiastic, easily impressed, and keen to impress others.

1) He's excited that Bill Tenner — a former workmate — has had a letter published in one of his magazines.
2) He's happy to welcome the newcomers. He plays euchre (a card game) with George. He shows off his knowledge of the big night out in town and particularly the best brothels.
3) He's the one who blurts out in anguish as they all wait for Carlson's gunshot to kill Candy's dog.
4) He's open about finding Curley's wife attractive — "Well, ain't she a looloo?"

There are Signs that Whit is already Doomed

There are already signs that things might get more grim for Whit.
In some ways he's already been tainted by the harsh ranch life:

1) He has sloping shoulders — as if he's carrying an invisible grain bag.
2) He's sad and nostalgic about the departed Bill Tenner.
3) He knows all about and recommends "old Susy's" brothel, going into quite a bit of detail — sounds like a favourite topic.

Whit seems to be...	
Naive	Enthusiastic
Hopeful	Brothel-crazy
Young	Doomed

Like the rest of the men, he's already screwing and boozing his money away.

Whit is Aware of what happens around him

1) He sees George's reasoning for arriving late — they don't have to work so long before Sunday's day off.
2) He sees there's a rivalry between Slim and Curley — and this is going to lead to trouble:
   "I seen her give Slim the eye. Curley never seen it."
3) He admires a man who is "handy". He's impressed by Curley's newspaper clippings about how he got into the final of the Golden Gloves (a boxing competition).

Whit likes to be in on any Action

Whit dashes out to see a possible fight between Slim and Curley, saying "Nobody knows what Slim can do." He's like a boy at school, running to see the fight in the playground.
But he misses out on the hunt for Lennie. He's made the messenger boy and is sent into town to get the deputy sheriff. So he's not at the scene of Lennie's death. He was probably really peeved.

Whit's doomed too — what, you couldn't see it coming?...

It's unlikely you'll be asked a question all about Whit, but you can't just forget about him. Like Carlson, he's needed to make the story work — he kind of fleshes out the book... Speaking of flesh, I had the biggest cheeseburger of my LIFE last night. All dripping with lard it was. Mmmm...

Slim

Slim is a powerful person on the ranch. But his power is limited. He's only powerful with day-to-day things like work. He can't do anything about the deaths of Curley's wife and Lennie.

Slim is the Top Bunkhouse Worker

1) He's a "jerkline skinner" (he controls a team of horses). This is a <u>very skilful</u> job.
2) He has a <u>natural air of authority</u> — "the prince of the ranch".
3) He's fit, healthy and good-looking — he attracts the attention of Curley's wife. He's the only person she addresses by name.
4) <u>Everyone likes him</u>. He's easy-going. His work-team is the best one to be on.

Prince of the Ranch, but looks a bit weird to me.

Slim is there at Key Moments

1) He <u>supports</u> Carlson at the crucial moment before Candy's dog is killed.
2) He <u>organises</u> Curley's trip to the doctor's when Lennie breaks his hand.
3) He <u>twice</u> says Lennie <u>has to be killed</u> at the end: "I guess we gotta get 'im."
4) He's the one who knows that it's George who has shot Lennie. It's Slim who <u>comforts George</u> — he sits down next to him, then takes him off for a drink.

Slim is the Spiritual leader of the men — he's "Godlike"

Slim is <u>different</u> from the other men. Steinbeck says he's "<u>Godlike</u>".

1) We're told "his slow speech had overtones not of thought, but of <u>understanding beyond thought</u>."
2) He has an instinctive understanding of the way <u>nature</u> works — the way life and death work. This is the <u>total opposite to Lennie</u>. Slim understands that <u>the weak do not survive</u> in nature.
3) Slim has "<u>dignity</u>" and is "<u>ageless</u>". The men understand this, on some level, and allow him to lead them.

<u>Slim</u> is...

Godlike	Majestic
Mysterious	Authority
Detached	Ageless

Slim's Not Cruel — but he is Practical

1) He's <u>not cruel</u>, even though he let Carlson shoot Candy's dog.
2) We might think drowning four of his own dog's puppies is cruel, but life is <u>very different</u> on a ranch. He simply says that "she couldn't feed that many." He <u>had to kill some</u> or else they would <u>all</u> have died.

Slim Accepts his own Fate and that of others

1) Like Candy and Crooks, Slim has accepted a <u>life of work</u> — he doesn't have a dream or escape plan.
2) He can do <u>nothing</u> about the deaths of Curley's wife or Lennie. Although he's "Godlike", he's not that powerful. However, he <u>could</u> have stopped Candy's dog being killed by Carlson, but <u>he chose not to</u>.
3) Most of the others get excited about something at some stage. He <u>never</u> does. He's <u>always calm</u>.

He's a <u>bright bloke</u>. Perhaps he sees it's <u>pointless</u> hoping for a better life. What a cheery bloke.

Slim's the ranch's God, or something like that...

The language Steinbeck uses to describe Slim is <u>mysterious</u>, and stands out from the more straight-forward stuff. e.g. Slim "moved with a majesty", and "his ear heard more than was said to him". Slim is different from the rest. Yeah, well, he still drowns ickle baby puppies. The big old meanie.

Curley's Wife

Curley's wife is the <u>only real woman</u> George and Lennie encounter. In some ways she is a bold and confident person (she's always strutting around and flirting). But in other ways she's <u>very fragile</u> (like when she's talking to Lennie at the end). One thing's for sure — she's <u>not happy</u>.

Curley's Wife is a Disruptive Influence

1) She's a woman in a <u>man's world</u> — and this messes things up.
2) All the men (apart from Slim) are wary of her. Perhaps she shows them what their own lives lack. Or maybe they know they're <u>tempted</u>, but they're aware of the <u>dangerous consequences</u> — both <u>physical</u> (from Curley), and <u>financial</u> (they'd probably lose their job).
3) But she doesn't leave them alone — she bursts into the bunkhouse <u>all the time</u>. She also intrudes on Crooks, Candy and Lennie when they're in Crooks' room.

> Curley's wife always seems to be looking for Curley — but maybe she's just looking for happiness, a way out.

The Men have Plenty to say about her

Everyone has <u>strong feelings</u> about Curley's wife. Some men are <u>attracted to her</u> (like Whit and Lennie) — and <u>others despise her</u> (like George and Candy).

1) Candy, Crooks and George all see her as <u>dangerous</u> and out of place on the farm. They call her "jailbait" and a "ratrap". This turns out to be true in one sense — Lennie is lured by her to his (and her) death.
2) Lennie is <u>dazzled</u> by her glamour and <u>soft beauty</u>. She is yet another soft thing he is <u>tempted to touch</u>. It can't be nice for her to be stared at by a random massive ranch hand like Lennie — "Lennie's eyes moved down her body, and though she did not seem to be looking at Lennie, she <u>bridled a little</u>".
3) Slim seems to enjoy her flirting. She calls him by his name, and he calls her "good-lookin'". He can <u>handle</u> her — maybe because he's not frightened of Curley (or maybe just because he's always calm).

After two weeks of marriage, Curley's wife is Unhappy

1) She <u>pretends</u> to be looking for Curley — but it seems as if really she's looking for the attention of the men, and some company.
2) She's bored by <u>Curley's boasts</u> about fighting. She doesn't actually believe half of it — and certainly not that he got his hand broken in a machine — she knows Lennie did it.
3) She only married Curley <u>on the rebound from losing her dream</u>.

And she's also Very Very Lonely

1) No one seems to love her — Curley's certainly not very affectionate (and his glove is <u>very seedy</u>).
2) She wants some <u>companionship</u> — "Think I don't like to talk to somebody ever' once in a while?".
3) She's "purty". She wears a lot of make-up and is proud of her hair — she uses her looks to get attention.
4) She's already <u>lost her own dream</u> of getting into the movies or going on stage.
5) Remember, she's married to Curley — what could possibly be <u>worse</u>. (Well, being shaken to death I guess...)

<u>Curley's Wife</u> is...	
Lonely	Fragile
"Purty"	Fed up
Young	Made-up

But she's Not Stupid

1) She's <u>well aware</u> of the power she holds over Curley and Candy (see page 11), and she's only been there for two weeks.
2) She <u>says</u> she <u>knows all about men</u> — they're "mutts". And she knows all about their need for dreams and about their need for drink.

Then again... she doesn't actually DO anything bad...

Curley's wife doesn't actually get involved with any of the men — even though the narrator and the characters say she's a tart and a flirt. Maybe she's just lonely and fed up living with a nutter of a husband. Which you would be — "glove fulla vaseline"... yuk. Don't write her off as just a tart.

Candy

Candy's story is <u>almost as depressing</u> as Lennie's. He's a victim of a <u>life of work</u>.
He's already <u>lost a hand</u>, and during the story he <u>loses his dog</u> and he <u>loses his dream</u>.

At the end he lays down and covers his eyes. In fact, it's near the end for him.
His body is <u>old and weak</u> — Curley's wife calls him a "<u>lousy ol' sheep</u>".

> *Candy* is...
>
> | | |
> |---|---|
> | Old | One-handed |
> | Friendly | Really old |
> | Lonely | Weak |

> *Think about Candy's name — his life definitely isn't sweet. And have a look at page 30 for more stuff about names.*

Candy Harms No-one — And he's Positive about others

1) Candy is the man who <u>welcomes George and Lennie</u> to the farm, showing them to their beds.
2) He's <u>patient</u> with George who's in a <u>foul mood</u> — he reassures him that his bed is free of lice.
3) He admires Curley for his fighting but <u>nothing else</u>. He likes the boss for the whisky he gave the men at Christmas — but he says he "gets pretty mad sometimes".
4) He befriends Lennie and George, and then Crooks (but only for a brief moment — see page 9) — their dream of a farm of their own <u>binds them together</u>.
5) In the end he realises Curley's wife is <u>more than just a "tart"</u> — he says she's a "Poor bastard".

He's Frail and Powerless — like his Dog

1) Candy is <u>old and weak</u>, and <u>disabled</u> — he lost his right hand (most people's strongest) in a machine on the farm. He gets <u>gut ache</u>, and he's always <u>scratching himself</u>. He's actually a bit of a <u>physical wreck</u>.
2) He has the <u>least respected job</u> of all the bunkhouse guys — the cleaner or "swamper" as it's called.
3) He's <u>not quite</u> one of the lads. For example, <u>no one</u> tries to save his dog from execution.
4) He's the one who's <u>left behind</u>. On workdays he stays behind to clean up. When the other men <u>go into town</u> on Saturday night, and when they go off to <u>lynch Lennie</u> — he's left behind.

And at the end he's left behind with <u>Curley's dead wife</u>, his <u>dead dream</u>, and memories of his <u>dead dog</u>.

He has a Weakness for Kidding Himself about things

1) Candy is all too quick to offer his compensation money to George so he can <u>join The Dream</u>.
2) He's a <u>desperate man</u> — he says he'll put them in his will even though he's only known them for one day.
3) It's because he wants to own something concrete. He doesn't want one of Slim's spare pups — he wants his <u>own dog</u>. He wants a share of his own land and animals with some economic value.

Poor Candy — he doesn't have any mates that'll shoot him...

It's a bit odd that Candy offers George and Lennie all his money when they've only just met. Then again, maybe it's the first chance to actually get out of the ranch since he lost his hand (four years ago). What a depressing thought — even though he had some money, he had nothing he could do with it. Then again, his dog was shot 10 minutes before. So it's not THAT surprising really...

Revision Summary — Characters

Well, they certainly are a cheery lot, aren't they? I'd just love to have them round for a party — Curley could try and fight everyone, Lennie could kill my girlfriend and then maybe Carlson could kill my dog... Oh great. Even less fun than that party though, is the prospect of going through this revision summary. I know, I know, but hey — the more you know about these guys, the more you can show them to be the losers they really are. So, here goes. You can refer back to the book to start off with, but eventually you have to be able to answer every single one of these questions on your own. And if you can't, the puppy-dog gets it...

1) Which of the following describes George better: a) small, quick, restless, strong and bony-nosed or b) fit, healthy, good-looking and easy-going?

2) Give three reasons which could help explain George's cynicism.

3) Name an animal that Lennie is described as. Why do you think Steinbeck describes Lennie as an animal?

4) When Lennie panics, does he: a) lose control of himself b) get mad or c) get scared? Explain your answer.

5) Which of these words best describes Carlson: a) tactless b) moody c) angry or d) hungry ?

6) Why doesn't anyone like Curley?

7) Give three reasons why the bunkhouse boys don't like Crooks.

8) Which of the following describes Whit: a) young and depressed or b) naive and enthusiastic?

9) Do either of the descriptions in the previous question apply to you? (D'oh if they do...)

10) Give three reasons why Slim stands out from the others on the ranch.

11) Describe what dreams Curley's wife has.

12) Do you think Candy is going to die old and miserable and alone? Explain your answer.

13) Give an example where George is kind to Lennie, and another where George is irritable towards Lennie. Find both examples in the first chapter of "Of Mice and Men".

14) Why do you think George is so worried from the very start about Curley's wife's presence on the farm?

15) Give three reasons why you think Lennie might like stroking or petting animals.

16) How do you think Lennie sees George?

17) Why do you think Carlson wants to shoot Candy's dog?

18) What do you think Curley's vaseline glove is supposed to say about Curley?

19) Say which of the following best describes Crooks, and explain why: a) he's proud and aloof and doesn't like any other people or b) he's really lonely and secretly longs for human companionship.

20) Why do you think Whit gets excited to see Bill Tenner's letter in the magazine?

21) Explain why you think the ranch men look up to Slim.

22) Suggest why Curley's wife is always out and about looking for Curley.

23) Write a paragraph saying why you think Candy offers Lennie and George all his money so that he can buy the farm with them.

24) Describe the role that Carlson plays in "Of Mice and Men".

25) What do you think Steinbeck is saying about racism in this book?

26) Do you think Whit is doomed to a life on the ranches? Explain your answer.

27) Explain whether you think Slim was right or wrong to let Carlson kill Candy's dog.

28) Is Curley's wife just a tart? Explain your answer.

29) Write a paragraph explaining Candy's importance in the book.

30) Why do you think George looks after Lennie?

31) Do you think that George is a pessimist or an optimist? Explain your answer.

32) Do you think Lennie is a bad man?

33) Say whether you agree or disagree with the following statement — 'Lennie is just a stupid guy who drains poor George's energy'. Explain your answer.

Ranch Life

Life on the ranch isn't much of a life — it's work. To survive, you have to stay out of trouble and keep yourself healthy enough to be able to work.

> 1) It's a man's world, with a definite hierarchy*.
> 2) There's a strict timetable and it's very competitive.
> 3) You live to work, and you always know who the boss is.
> 4) It's a fighting culture — the mob rules.

I done another bad thing

All the men Know Their Place

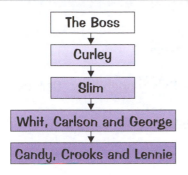

The Boss
↓
Curley
↓
Slim
↓
Whit, Carlson and George
↓
Candy, Crooks and Lennie

1) The boss wears spurs and rides a horse. Candy says he gave them whisky last Christmas, but that he shouts a lot. The boss just supervises the ranch.
2) Curley is no. 2, but only because he's the boss's son. No one likes him and they know he'll never get fired (Candy mentions this). He's a nightmare.
3) Slim's good at his job. The men respect him and even Curley is a bit afraid of him. He tells Curley not to get Lennie fired after his hand gets crushed.
4) After them it's a bit of a mix, depending on how old, healthy and new you are. Crooks could be last because he's black, but he can still wind Lennie up. Then again, Crooks isn't even allowed into the bunkhouse, but Lennie is.

The whole farm is like a Machine for work

1) The farm is a series of spaces — all clearly defined. It's all functional and simple with no luxuries — just the farmhouse, the barn and the bunkhouse. It's not beautiful like the riverside.
2) The bunkhouse is a cross between a boarding school dormitory and a jail. There's just a stove, a manky bed each, a table and some boxes to sit on.
3) The men aren't encouraged to own anything — they don't have identities apart from how much they can work, or how much they fight.
4) Their "play" times are also really strict and laid out clearly. They play cards inside and horseshoes outside. On Saturday nights they go into town and then they have Sundays off.
5) They don't have their own lives at all. They just work. To put it bluntly, they're all basically homeless, unless they can make themselves useful somewhere like this awful ranch.

Men are Not Machines

Men are not machines — they're flesh and blood with lots of strengths and lots of weaknesses. This is one of the most important messages in the book.

1) Ranch life is not healthy. It's not natural to work men like animals.
2) Ranch life destroys men's dreams, and can end in injury (Crooks, Candy) or death (Lennie, Curley's wife).
3) Lennie is the perfect example of this. He's really strong and does whatever he's told without thinking about it. And look at what happens to him in the end. That's right. He dies. A lot.

'Of Mice and Men' raises lots of issues, but this is one of the key points Steinbeck is making —

> Men should not be treated like dumb animals

Men aren't dumb animals — at least not before puberty...

Bill Tenner moved on from this ranch — why should we care? Because he's a reminder that some people have had the sense to get the hell out of dodge. It's significant that he wrote a letter too — it means a move out of the hard physical labour into more articulate, thoughtful life. Smart move.

*a hierarchy is a way of ranking people according to status or authority.

Shooting Candy's Dog

This incident is important, trust me. It's not just one of a series of violent incidents in the book.

> 1) Candy's old dog stinks.
> 2) Carlson persuades him to have it killed.
> 3) Candy reluctantly agrees, and the dog is shot.

"a drag-footed sheep dog, gray of muzzle, and with pale, blind old eyes"

Carlson kills Candy's old dog

1) Carlson schemes to get the dog shot.
2) He does this by breaking down Candy's defences.
3) He pretends it's for the sake of the animal — but it's not really.
   He doesn't want to sleep in the same room as the dog. His motives are selfish.
4) Carlson offers to kill the dog himself. He offers one of Slim's pups as a replacement.
   But this isn't out of kind-heartedness — he just wants to get the job done.
5) He points at the spot in the dog's neck with his boot where he'll shoot him — he's thoughtless. Callous.
6) He leads the dog out with a leather strap — it's like the dog's noose.
   Nooses make us think of hangings... the poor dog is being lead to its own execution.

Slim has the Authority to save the dog but Does Nothing

1) Carlson gets the help of Slim. This is important — Slim has the say
   over most things. Slim has the power to save the dog, but he doesn't.
2) It's Slim who can offer another pup. And it's Slim who, at the end,
   reminds Carlson to take a shovel to bury it.
3) Slim is being practical. But he's still cruel in a way — he doesn't
   consider Candy's feelings. He just says, "Carl's right".

Now I've got a dead dawg...

Candy is Useless like his dog

1) Candy has had his dog from a pup — the dog is his best friend.
2) He's clearly upset and fights to keep it.
3) But... he himself is old and weak, and disabled. Just like his dog.
4) Afterwards he regrets letting Carlson shoot it. He wishes he'd done it instead.

It's a Cruel World on the Ranch

1) There's no mercy on the ranch for animals or humans — it's one of the messages of the book.
2) When animals and people no longer serve a purpose they're got rid of. Slim drowns most of his pups
   — no one bats an eyelid about this. No one defends Candy or helps him save his dog.

Candy has one hand, and is old and fragile like his dog. He might think he could be next.
He'd be right — they could all be next. The men are just like animals labouring on the farm.

If anyone shot my dog I'd pull their head off...

This bit of the book really shows the cruelty of life on the ranch. Maybe not so much that an old
and ill dog is being shot — more that no one cares how Candy is feeling. The men are treated and
behave like animals. Sounds like school to me... being herded round the place and then fed swill.

Hands

This is a page about hands. It could prove to be really handy. Ho ho ho. No seriously, most of the characters' hands are mentioned, so Steinbeck's definitely trying to say something with them...

> To survive in the tough world of the 1930s ranches you needed —
> 1) a good pair of hands to <u>work</u>.
> 2) a good pair of hands to <u>fight</u> — when necessary.
> This is a competitive male world — it's survival of the fittest...

Curley

1) He is described as "handy". He's a small man but an excellent boxer and is always trying to prove it.
2) But he also keeps one of his hands soft for his wife — one hand for <u>loving</u>, the other for <u>fighting</u>.
3) Lennie <u>crushes</u> his fighting hand, so can't fight any more. This makes him even <u>less</u> of a man.

Candy

1) Candy's missing a hand. That's a huge <u>drawback</u> as they <u>have</u> to do physical work.
2) The only reason he has a job at all is because he lost his hand "right here on this ranch".
3) If he ever got fired, he'd be homeless and <u>useless</u>. No wonder he wants to join George and Lennie.

Now I know how the mouse feels...

Lennie

Lennie has those famous hands — heavy "pendula" hands.
1) They're <u>amazing</u> for farmwork.
2) They love "petting" soft things.
3) They don't know their own <u>strength</u> and usually kill the things they pet.

George

1) He may have small hands but we're told they are "<u>strong</u>".
2) He's teamed up with Lennie — this <u>compensates</u> for his small hands.
3) Together, he and Lennie make the perfect team — good at hard work (Lennie), but also smart and ambitious (George).

Slim

1) He has hands which are both "large" and "lean". They're like those of a "temple dancer".
2) They're just like Slim — "delicate" and respected. Everyone looks up to him because of such qualities.

Curley's Wife

1) Her hands are part of her <u>sexiness</u>. She polishes her nails in front of Crooks, Lennie and Candy and puts "her hands on her hips". This is a confrontational and come-and-get-me-if-you-dare gesture.
2) When she demonstrates to Lennie her ability to act in the barn, she does so with her hands. Her hands aren't about fighting — but they are about <u>getting what she wants</u> and fulfilling her dreams...

Edward Scissorhands eat your heart out

Hand over that rifle — I'm hunting wabbits...

Lennie's hands are both destructive and affectionate. They stroke and pet first, then they crush, destroy and smother — mice, a puppy, then Curley's wife. He's not aware of what he is capable of — petting and smothering get all mixed up in his big dopey hands. Lovely lovely lovely...

Names and Titles

Names are really important — Steinbeck uses them to drop hints about the characters.

Lots of the men's names Describe their Characters

1) <u>Curley</u> — he's just like his curly hair — tense and wound up tight, like a spring.
2) <u>Slim</u> — he's tall and elegant, like his name.
3) <u>Crooks</u> — he's got a crooked back.
4) <u>Candy</u> — ironic name. His life is anything but sweet.
5) <u>Whitey</u> — he was the blacksmith obsessed with being clean. It's a joke. Honest.
6) <u>Whit</u> and <u>Carlson</u> are just average guys. The American Dictionary says that "whit" means "the smallest part or particle imaginable" and that "carl" is "a man of the common people".

1) Lennie's surname is "<u>Small</u>". Carlson makes a joke about it. But Lennie's really huge. Ho ho...
2) Plus, Lennie is fairly 'small' in the brains department, so in a way, "small" is <u>right</u>, even though he's huge.
3) George's surname is "Milton". I don't think it's meant to mean anything. George is the central character, so maybe Steinbeck wants us to think about him as a <u>real person</u>, not a stereotype... maybe.

Curley's Wife has No Name

1) She wants <u>recognition</u>, <u>attention</u>, <u>her own identity</u>, and her <u>own life</u>.
   To emphasise how she has none of these things, Steinbeck doesn't even give her a <u>name</u>.
2) Even the <u>prostitutes</u> in Soledad have a name — and a definite role. But <u>not</u> Curley's wife.
3) She is just someone's "<u>wife</u>" — no identity of her own. Without him she really would be nothing.
   What a <u>miserable</u> life. Marrying someone you <u>don't like</u> and then losing your own identity completely.

The Place Names are Meaningful

<u>Soledad</u> is the local town. In Spanish it means "<u>loneliness</u>".

1) You could say <u>all</u> the characters here are <u>lonely</u>.
2) They work in teams but are all out <u>on their own</u>.
3) Those that start off together get <u>split up</u> (Curley and wife, George and Lennie, Candy and dog).

<u>Weed</u> is where George and Lennie have come from, where Lennie did a "bad thing".

1) A weed is a plant you <u>don't want</u>. It <u>deprives</u> nice plants of <u>space</u> and <u>food</u>.
2) The memory of the "bad thing" <u>spoils</u> their new life. Yuck.

These aren't made up names — they're <u>real places</u>. Steinbeck's keeping it as <u>realistic</u> as possible.

The novel's title is Very Revealing

...and you're absolutely sure that this sausage is part of the plan?

"Of Mice and Men" is a quote from a Robert Burns poem:

The best laid schemes o' mice and men
Gang aft agley ⟵ This means "often go wrong".
And leave us nought but grief and pain
For promised joy.

It tells us not to expect anyone to be happy, and that plans <u>always</u> fail — no matter how well they're "laid" or thought out. The title is a constant reminder that <u>failure is inevitable</u>. Oh great...

The thin mouse got away — what a narrow squeak...

The ones I feel sorry for are the animals. I mean, poor old Candy's dog didn't even know what was coming — it doesn't have a name either. "Candy's dog" and "Curley's wife" — they're both given names suggesting that they 'belong' to someone else. Euch. Not good for your morale...

The Battle of the Sexes

There's not many women in this novel, but they are important. Understanding their roles will help you work out more about the other characters. Then of course there's Lennie's stroking fetish...

There are Three Types of women in the novel

Curley's Wife

1) Her only weapon is her sexuality — the men fancy her, but call her a "God damn tramp".
2) She haunts the farm like a ghost — "Jesus Christ, Curley's wife can move quiet" (Candy, Chapter 4).
3) She has her own impossible dreams of being a movie star, and she's actually pretty naive.
4) She's like the men in a way — dreaming of another life and frustrated by the reality of her own.

Lennie's Aunt Clara

1) Clara had a huge impact on Lennie as an authority figure. This is shown pretty clearly when Lennie imagines being told off by her in the final chapter (just before he sees a giant rabbit).
2) The impression we get of Clara from George is that she was a mixture of kindness and strictness, but in Lennie's head she's someone who makes him feel bad, inadequate and dependent on George.

Susy in Soledad

1) Susy runs a brothel that most of the men go to on Saturday nights.
2) Whit says it's the best one because the girls are "clean", Susy has a sense of humour and they don't put pressure on the men.
3) This is the opposite to Curley's wife, who is always pressurising the men.

1) With Aunt Clara, it's not about sex.
2) With Susy, it's no-strings attached and business-like.
3) But Curley's wife is a dangerous, sexy, demanding 'real' woman that the men struggle to deal with.

Lennie has been in Trouble with women Before

1) George is wary of Curley's wife because he's scared Lennie will get in trouble, like on their last job.
2) He's certain Lennie doesn't do anything "in meanness" but only wants "to touch ever'thing he likes" like velvet, or a puppy's fur.
3) Everyone who finds out about this seems okay with it (though reluctantly at first), but if you ask me it's got more sexual undertones than a Barry White song.

The men and women Don't Understand each other

1) The men assume Curley's wife is a tart — George says "She's a rat-trap if ever I seen one."
2) She, in turn, assumes the men are basically useless — she says "I seen too many you guys."
3) Only Susy comes close to understanding these men. "I know what you boys want" she says — cheap sex, whisky and an easy life. BUT this is a stereotype too...

In the novel, men stereotype women, and women stereotype men. They put each others' dreams down and make it hard for the other to achieve anything.

When you're stuck like glue — Vaseline...

What's going on with Curley's glove? It implies that he has mixed feelings about women — he wants to enjoy them (soft hand), but also control them (rough hand). Hmmm... bit sick if you ask me.

Loneliness

Now, I think this one is really important. Steinbeck himself gave us a big hint by calling the nearby town "Soledad". This means "loneliness" in Spanish. Clever, eh?

> 1) Slim says ranch workers "get so they don't want to talk to nobody".
> 2) George says ranch guys "are the loneliest in the world".
> 3) Crooks says "A guy needs somebody — to be near him".
> 4) And he also says "A guy goes nuts if he ain't got nobody.
>   Don't make no difference who the guy is, long's he's with you."

Everyone on the Ranch is Lonely...

1) All the bunkhouse men are single — so they're pretty likely to be lonely.
2) They're like orphans. George says "They got no family".
3) They've got nothing to look forward to, except work for the rest of their lives.
4) George plays solitaire — a game for one.
5) Lennie and George look after each other, but George still feels lonely.
6) It's like an unequal marriage, where George has all the responsibility.
   Others find it strange that they travel around together.

Curley

Curley is still lonely even though he's married — he's failed miserably. His marriage isn't working — the only time we see him with his wife is when she's dead. This rams home the point about this disastrous marriage.

Curley's Wife

She's not happy living in her father–in–law's house. She thinks she has missed opportunities by living with Curley and this band of lonely men. She tries to get a bit of companionship by flirting with them and talking to them.

Crooks

And Crooks, the stable-buck, lives all alone — he's exiled from the others, mainly because he's black. And he's wary of them — when Lennie pays him a surprise visit Crooks doesn't seem to want his company. He's used to loneliness — and even prefers it.

...and No One can think of an Answer

1) The bunkhouse guys blow their money every Saturday night on whores and booze
   at "Susy's Place"— but it doesn't stop them being lonely.
2) Lennie and George think that having their own place would solve EVERYTHING.
   But George knows it isn't going to happen. It's just a dream and this depresses him.
3) Lennie has his animals. That's a kind of solution for him. At least until he kills them.
   Candy has his dog. Or at least did until Carlson shot it. Depressing stuff...

And when anyone tries to grab hold of someone else it can end in disaster. Curley's marriage, for example. Or Lennie holding his animals, holding the girl's skirt in Weed, holding on to Curley's wife. He has a real need for companionship.

I'd be lonely if I worked in the middle of nowhere...

It's no wonder this lot are lonely really, is it? I mean, stuck out in the sticks with a bunch of nutters, no hope of getting out and nothing to look forward to — sounds pretty depressing to me. This book is so depressing... I think I'm going to have to... sniff sniff... yes... eat more chocolate.

Doomed to Failure

Nobody actually says "everybody's <u>doomed</u>" (because they're mostly <u>too thick</u> to notice). But they <u>are</u>. There's no way out and no one gets to fulfil any dreams. What a downer...

> *This is a list of things that are doomed in this novel. Pretty depressing.*
> *1)* *Loving relationships between men and women.*
> *2)* *Racial harmony.*
> *3)* *Any dream had by anyone. Ever.*
> *4)* *Quality of life.*
> *5)* *Any mouse in the surrounding area.*

oh great...

Lennie is *Particularly Doomed*

1) Lennie is often <u>violent</u>. That violence is often <u>unintended</u>. But it still gets him into <u>trouble</u>:
   — holding that girl's dress in Weed,
   — squashing mice and the puppy... (and not forgetting killing Curley's wife).
2) According to George it's not because Lennie's mean, it's because he "don't know no rules".
3) <u>But</u>, Lennie also has sudden <u>fits of anger</u> — e.g. hurling the puppy across the barn after he's killed it.
4) This suggests that maybe Lennie isn't <u>quite</u> as innocent and blameless as George says he is.
5) Also, people <u>pick on</u> Lennie because he's stupid. Curley picks on him as soon as they meet. So does the boss, Curley's wife, and Crooks. His <u>stupidity</u> gets him in constant trouble.
6) Because he can't think for himself, he lives by his senses. That's partly where the stroking comes in. He <u>knows</u> it *feels* nice — he doesn't wonder why, he just <u>does it</u>. Doom, doom, doom, doom, doom...

George knows that *Trouble* is *Inevitable*

George gets tired of describing their dream farm because he <u>doesn't really believe it</u> deep down. When he sees Curley's wife dead, he admits that "I think I knowed <u>from the very first</u>" that the dream would never come true. It was inevitable. Doomed, doomed, doomed, doomed...

1) That's why he tells Lennie to keep his <u>mouth shut</u>.
2) That's why he makes an emergency plan to meet Lennie by the pool.
3) He says "if you jus' happen to get in trouble <u>like you always done</u> before". You can tell he thinks Lennie <u>will</u> get in trouble again because he goes on about how he's <u>always</u> done it before — like a parent.
4) He's wary of Curley's wife straight away and knows she will be involved somehow.

No one is *Happy* at the end of the novel

No one ends up happy or fulfilled. They're all doomed, doomed, doomed, doomed, doomed...

1) <u>George</u> kills <u>Lennie</u> after Lennie kills <u>Curley's wife</u>, so none of them are happy (especially the dead ones).
2) <u>Candy's</u> not going to get to share the dream farm with George, and his dog's been shot.
3) <u>Crooks</u> is still treated as an inferior because of his skin colour.
4) <u>Curley's</u> good hand is knackered so he can't win fist fights anymore and his pretty wife is dead.
5) <u>Whit</u> and <u>Carlson</u> are both idiots anyway, who aren't ever truly happy or unhappy...
6) <u>Slim</u> remains devoid of emotion. He just cleans up after it all happens...

Oh what joy. Think I might just pop off and kill myself now. Then again, it *is* Eastenders tonight...

Doom comes to us all — especially the mice...

I've just thought, one person might be happy — the boss. I mean, he can just hire someone else. Who cares what the men get up to as long as the work gets done. There you go. Life is harsh, unless you're on top of the pile. No one else has a chance. Oh great. So glad I read this book...

Dreams

You'll have gathered by now that no-one in the book is TRULY happy. Everyone's <u>missing something</u>. None of them own their own land or home (except the boss). All any of them have are their dreams...

This novel is all about <u>The American Dream</u> —
1) America is meant to be a land built on <u>promise</u> and <u>opportunity</u>.
2) It promised <u>independence</u>, <u>land</u> and a <u>decent living</u> through honest work.
3) It also means, in theory, that <u>anyone</u> could become <u>successful</u>.
4) Trouble is, in <u>practice</u>, most people need to be <u>born rich</u> to make it.
5) It's a great dream for the lucky few that succeed, but <u>horrible for the rest</u>.

What's my dream?

People on the ranch are going <u>Nowhere</u>

1) The ranch is for men who <u>spend</u> all their money "in some lousy cat-house" (a brothel) then just "work another month" and get another $50 to waste somewhere.
2) The ones who just stay on the ranch <u>won't ever have enough</u> money to be able to move on in life.
3) Whit and Carlson are <u>average</u> guys. They're physically fit, and are able to make enough money to buy themselves the basic whisky and sex they want. They have <u>no ambitions</u> in life.
4) You might say that because they have no dreams, they're never truly happy or unhappy. They're just <u>there</u>.

George and Lennie dream of <u>A Better Life</u>

George and Lennie are <u>different</u> — they don't want to work on ranches every day until they die.

1) The dream of the farm keeps George and Lennie going during their tough times — and it <u>infects</u> others, like Candy and Crooks.
2) But it was <u>never really</u> going to happen. Steinbeck says "each mind was popped into the future when this lovely thing should come about." It's all in a <u>pretend future</u> — not in the <u>real present</u>.
3) George says "I got to thinking maybe we would". Maybe that's just because Lennie liked hearing it so much. The American Dream is nothing but a <u>cruel trick</u>. If you fall for it, you're <u>doomed</u>.

That's what Steinbeck is saying — the American Dream is <u>just a dream</u>.

The trouble with dreams is that they're <u>Not Real</u>

1) George and Lennie's dream is just a bunch of <u>words</u> repeated over and over.
2) They start off being said "rhythmically", but by the end they're spoken "<u>monotonously</u>" when George finally accepts that dreams don't come true — the dream becomes a <u>burden</u> to him.
3) Lennie just wants to be able to "tend the rabbits". It's George who <u>thought up</u> the dream.
4) George has other dreams, but the farm is the only one that's truly idyllic — because it's <u>impossible</u>.

<u>George's Other Dreams</u>

Having a girl   Playing cards and pool
Having an easy life
Panning for gold

George's <u>Dreams Die</u> with Lennie

1) When George kills Lennie, George is <u>resigned</u> to the life of the single man.
2) Even though it'll be "an easy life" without Lennie around, it's <u>not</u> the paradise farm he <u>secretly wanted</u>.
3) When George kills Lennie, he is also killing off <u>his own chance</u> of real happiness.

Steinbeck is saying that <u>normal people's dreams don't come true</u>.

Life is but a dream — and I'm stuck on Elm Street...

Crooks is very cynical about these dreams. He's been there and done that. His family owned land, then they lost it. He gets swept up in it for a second, then Curley's wife comes in and threatens him. So there's a little bit of hope but then it gets crushed. Great... that's really cheered my winter up...

Why George Kills Lennie

Bet you never thought George would kill his best friend. You need to try and understand why, to understand what the book is saying. It's a bit painful, but I know you'll cope...

> These are the options George thinks about after Lennie kills Curley's wife:
> 1) Prison — maybe Lennie will be taken to prison and be treated well.
> 2) Lynching — Curley and the crew will kill Lennie when they find him.
> 3) Find a cave — Lennie could run away and live in a cave on his own.

You may take my rabbits, but you will never take my freedom...

All the Options are Bad

There's no good solution:

1) Slim refers to the jail as a "cage", saying "That ain't no good, George."
2) Prison might be okay if George finds Lennie first, but like Slim says, "Curley's gonna want to shoot 'im". There's not much hope of getting Lennie safely into the hands of the law.
3) The lynching is obviously bad. Lennie would die a horrible death, tortured by Curley and the others. Curley wants to "shoot for his guts" — an agonising way to die that would take hours.
4) Lennie's not smart enough to run away and take care of himself — we've already seen him drink dirty water and George says "the poor bastard'd starve".

Lennie's Death is Inevitable

This time Lennie has really "done a bad thing". A whoopsie of the highest degree.
We're not talking dresses and puppies, we're talking actual death of a real human being.

1) George doesn't even consider them going on the run together again, like when they left Weed.
2) George knows that Lennie can't get away with it this time — "We can't let 'im get away".

Lennie's fate is sealed when Curley's wife dies. He'll be lynched, unless George does something.

George Has to Kill Lennie

1) George doesn't want Lennie to get lynched — it's a horrible, undignified way to die. He'll be hunted like an animal and murdered without a trial and without justice. He'll be in agony, and no one will help him.
2) Instead, George takes control. Lennie's death is inevitable, so George decides it's better to kill him himself, humanely. Bit of a big decision to have to make.
3) Remember when Candy's dog got shot? Well, afterwards Candy said "I shouldn't ought to of let no stranger shoot my dog." He regrets his dog died an undignified death at the hands of a stranger.
4) George doesn't make the same mistake. He deliberately steals Carlson's gun so that he can kill Lennie.

Death is Lennie's new Dream

1) George wants Lennie to die happy. It's so tragic. He "monotonously" repeats the dream to Lennie.
2) The story ends by the river, where it began, with Lennie close to George, trusting George to protect him.
3) George's voice is "almost business-like", and he knows he has to do it. He hears the others coming.
4) This mercy killing is totally different from a mob lynching.
5) Slim says it all — "You hadda, George. I swear you hadda." And he did. To let Lennie die with dignity.

Death — almost worse than a Doner Kebab...

Is George just being selfish? I guess you could say that he is. He'll be free. But wouldn't it be more selfish to let Lennie die a horrible death when he knows he can let him die without pain or indignity? I mean, yes he'll have an "easy life", but will he ever get over it? I have my doubts...

Interpreting Things

This page is about making links between different things in the book — it's about spotting similarities. Think of it this way — just about everything in this novel has a meaning.

Nature has its own Dark Side

1) The area by the pool seems idyllic — there's no work, no bunkhouse, no dead dogs, no boss.
2) There's water to drink, wood for a fire, and it's really beautiful — the water has "slipped twinkling over the yellow sands in the sunlight". Ah. How nice.
3) But, nature is also quite scary. There are watersnakes, and herons that eat the watersnakes, and then coyotes that would eat the heron given half a chance — it's survival of the fittest, like everywhere else.
4) The idea that nature is a paradise is an illusion. The water looks nice, but George warns that it looks "scummy". Lennie wants to live in a cave but he'd never survive in the harsh reality of nature.

Candy is like his Dog

Yes he is. Four legs. Wet nose. Funny odours... Just kidding — well, not completely...

1) Candy is old and crippled, like his dog.
2) Candy's dog looks up hopefully when someone enters the bunkhouse. This is just like Candy's reaction to the arrival of George and Lennie, and the feeling of hope he gets from their dream.
3) Slim says "I wish somebody'd shoot me if I get old an' a cripple". Thing is, Candy is himself old, and a cripple. Should Candy just be put out of his misery too? What about Crooks — he's also crippled...
4) Curley's wife says the "whole country is fulla mutts". "Mutts" are mongrels. She's talking about dogs. Steinbeck is talking about men. The whole country's full of no-hopers like the bunch on this ranch.

Candy's dog is more than just a dog. When it gets shot, it's like Steinbeck is saying that the old and the weak get put down by society. We'll all be metaphorically shot in the head one day...

> Metaphors are used to describe one thing as if it were another. And they never use "like" or "as".
>
> Example: Candy's dog could be a metaphor for old age.

Twix, please

Red is the Magic Colour

Red is pretty much the only colour mentioned on the drab ranch — it stands out. Red is...
1) The colour of danger, warning and bloodshed. It's also associated with sex, so sex = danger.
2) The only colour used to describe Curley's wife — lips, nails, and red "feathers" on her "red mules".
3) The colour of the girl's dress Lennie clung to in Weed. This gives Lennie's stroking fetish a sexual side.

The Cards are also symbolic

how much was yours then?

1) George plays solitaire. It's a one-man game.
2) Lennie picks up a card and wonders why it looks the same both ways up. "That's jus' the way they make 'em" George replies. He's saying that you can't change what is inevitable. Just like Lennie's death. It's poignant that Lennie's asking, and George gives the answer. Sound familiar to anyone?

What does being shot in the head remind me of — ah yes, life...

Something else — I know it's only a little thing, but it's quite neat. Crooks has a pair of gold-rimmed glasses, and he's the only guy to have many possessions. He's wise, and sees a lot (hence the glasses, boom boom). You could even say he sees through people, so he winds them up...

Revision Summary

Well, this is certainly a cheery book, isn't it? It's so cheery I think I might just go home and stop breathing... Still, at least there's lots to write about. If you manage to get through these questions, it'll mean that you understand what the heck Steinbeck was on about. It is very depressing, but I reckon it's a pretty touching story — very human. And certainly not the kind of fluffy stuff you find on 'Neighbours'... I mean, there's swearing and EVERYthing...

1) Write a list of all the characters you can think of, putting them in order of importance (I mean importance in the ranch's hierarchy*). Start at the top, putting the boss first.
2) Explain why Crooks is at the bottom of the ranch's hierarchy.
3) Why do you think Steinbeck chose 'Soledad' to be the nearby town?
4) Why does Carlson kill Candy's dog?
5) Write a couple of lines saying why the colour red is important in the book.
6) In what ways does Candy resemble his dog?
7) What kind of dog would you be and why?
8) Say what is noticeable about each of these characters' hands: a) Lennie b) Candy and c) Slim.
9) Curley fills his glove with vaseline — write a couple of lines explaining why you think he does this and what this says about him.
10) Why do you think Steinbeck bothers with all these descriptions of hands?
11) Do you think Lennie's desire to stroke soft things is an innocent one? Give three reasons why you think that.
12) For each of these characters, explain what their name represents (or why it is important): a) Curley b) Slim c) Crooks d) Candy e) Whit.
13) Write a paragraph to explain why you think Slim lets Carlson kill Candy's dog.
14) Where does the title of the book "Of Mice and Men" actually come from?
15) What does the title tell us about what's inside the book?
16) Who was Aunt Clara and why is she important?
17) What (apart from the crudely obvious) do you think is the attraction of the brothel for the bunkhouse boys?
18) What do you think the guys' general opinion of women is in this book?
19) Write a paragraph about the way Steinbeck writes about nature in "Of Mice and Men".
20) Why do you think Bill Tenner's letter is mentioned?
21) Do you think it's significant that George always plays solitaire? Why?
22) Explain why each of the following characters is lonely. Write a short paragraph for each one: a) Curley b) Curley's wife c) Crooks and d) George.
23) One of the messages of the books seems to be "Men should not be treated like dumb animals". Do you agree with this? Write a couple of paragraphs saying why.
24) Is Lennie mean? Give at least five decent points to back up your opinion.
25) Why do you think George and Lennie want to own their own farm?
26) Do you think having dreams is important for the characters in the book? Why?
27) What's your dream?
28) Why do you think George kills Lennie?
29) If you had been in George's place, do you think you would have killed Lennie?
30) Write an alternative ending to "Of Mice and Men" (i.e. so that George doesn't kill Lennie) — it can be anything you like, but it has to be realistic (no flying elephants or machine-gun-wielding goats or anything).

*a hierarchy is a way of ranking people according to status or authority.

The Structure

"Structure" is just a fancy word for the way that Steinbeck planned and wrote the novel — it's the author's design. It's good to step back and try and get an idea of the big picture.

Nature Starts and Ends the novel

The novel is balanced — it starts and ends outdoors at the pool. It starts with life and dreams, and ends in death and, er... well, more death. The stuff in between takes place indoors on the ranch.

1) The whole ranch belongs to the boss — no one else on that ranch can call it their home.
2) The interiors are all pretty sparse ("white-washed", "small, square windows" etc...) and unfriendly.
3) It's not a welcoming, healthy environment for dreamers like Lennie and George. They don't belong there.
4) We know Lennie is described as an animal — it's appropriate that he dies out in nature.

One of the novel's messages is that having a dream goes against the laws of nature.

1) Slim knows it, George learns it and by the end of the book the reader knows it too.
2) That could be why the book starts and ends outdoors — survival of the fittest rules the world.
3) Or maybe it's just a kind of primeval innocence — a garden of Eden where man hasn't ruined anything yet.

Nothing goes right for George and Lennie

Is Nature good or bad?
1) It's a pretty, utopian dream...
2) ...Like a return to innocence.
3) But it's eerie and powerful.
4) And it's survival of the fittest.

It's been a bit of a rollercoaster ride for George and Lennie. Poor old fellers...

1) They switch from hope to despair, from moments of happiness to moments of grim pessimism, and from big rows to sharing a dream for their future.
2) Whenever they think they're getting a break, it ends up going badly for them. It happened in Weed, it happens at this ranch too. George hints that it's happened a lot before — "All the time somethin' like that."
3) This time they definitely hit rock bottom though. George crashes to reality. Lennie ends up six feet under.

And while they're going up and down, the violence is building up all the time:

dead mice ⟹ dead dog ⟹ crushed hand ⟹ dead girl ⟹ dead Lennie

AND it's the most depressing book in the world... Did I mention that yet?

It's a Novel written like a Play

The year after he wrote "Of Mice and Men", Steinbeck adapted it to make it a play. It's all very visual, and very dramatic.

1) This works well because the entrances and exits are some of the key moments in the novel.
2) Each chapter has just one location. And it all takes place over one long weekend. So it's easy to stage.
3) The location descriptions at the beginning of each chapter are like instructions to a stage designer — they're very specific and give the reader a definite visual image of where the action takes place.

The characters also have specific, visual qualities:

1) There's Curley's wife and her bright red accessories.
2) And it looks pretty cool having a little guy like George yelling at a mammoth like Lennie.
3) Leading Candy's dog out to be shot is pretty effective too.

I read Steinbeck therefore I am — fairly depressed...

A long weekend isn't a huge amount of time for a whole story. And Lennie dies on a Sunday. It's meant to be a day of rest. And no one seems to go to church. They just wander about playing horseshoes and killing puppies and shooting their best friends in the head... Not very churchy...

The Language

Real people use real language. We speak in our own accents using the dialect and slang words which people around us know and use. Steinbeck wrote in the language of real people in 1930s California.

The Language is trying to be Realistic

People who sound dumb can still have brains...

1) The bunkhouse guys aren't that stupid. They're literate — they read magazines.
2) Crooks even reads a law book. But his language is just as bad as the others' — he says things like "I ain't so crippled I can't work like a son-of-a-bitch if I want to."
3) So their language DOESN'T automatically express ignorance.
4) Some of it's pretty harsh — there are a lot of racist references to Crooks as a "nigger". This isn't because Steinbeck's trying to be offensive — he's just captured a moment in time, in a society that was racist.

There are a few Weird Words about Work...

The words for what work you'd do on a ranch sound a bit weird, but this is what they mean:

1) The best job is a "jerkline skinner" (like Slim) — in control of a team of mules (or horses) pulling a wagon.
2) You'd almost certainly find yourself "pounding your tail" and "bustin' a gut"— working ridiculously hard. "Bucking grain" (filling and loading sacks) would probably do your back in.
3) A "cultivator" is a big farm machine to help break up the soil. A "Jackson fork" is a mechanical hay fork.
4) You'd look forward to your "jack" (pay) at the end of the month, but it wouldn't be much.
5) And if you were no longer fit and healthy you may have one of the marginal jobs like "swamper" — cleaner and general 'menial chores' guy. If you were a "stable buck" you'd be in charge of the horses and mules.

And a Load of Weird Words about "Play"

1) In the evenings you could play "euchre" — a card game.
2) At the weekend you could go to the local "flop-house" or "cat-house" (a brothel) and pay for your "crack" (sex). Or just have a couple of "shots of corn" (a double whisky).
3) If you'd chosen the "crack" though, you'd hope to avoid getting "bow-legged" or "burned" (an STI) from your particular "floosy" (prostitute).
4) If you were lucky, she'd have been "purty" (pretty) and "clean"— disease-free.
5) If you were unlucky you may have "blown your stake" — spent all your wages / savings.

The Cat House

There are loads of Other Odd Words

Some Random Words About This
1) *"canned" — getting sacked.*
2) *going on the "county" — being dependent on miserly, demeaning state handouts.*
3) *getting "greybacks" or "pants rabbits" — lice from unhygienic working or living conditions.*

Some Random Words About That
1) *"hoosegow" — prison.*
2) *the "booby hatch" — the lunatic asylum.*
3) *"bum steer" — wrong information.*

Insults — less painful than the injury they're added to...

Curley's wife refers to the guys in Crooks' room as "bindle bums" and "bindle stiffs". Well, a bindle is a bedroll (or a sleeping bag, to you and me). So bindle bums are basically tramps who don't move further than their bed. So that's me then, especially at the weekend. Ah... the weekend... ah...

Cool Background Stuff

Steinbeck thought a writer should only be judged on the work he did. But I think it's good to know more about him — because it'll help to understand some of what's in the book... hopefully.

Steinbeck was Born in the Salinas Valley

John Steinbeck was born in 1902 in the Salinas valley. The places in the book really exist — in California in the west of the United States. He wasn't making them up.

1) He often worked on ranches whilst on school holidays — so he knew the life.
2) He loved animals, had daily contact with them when he was growing up, and kept a dog.
3) His parents had some land — he was a rural kid.

Then he became Famous

After "Of Mice and Men" was published, Steinbeck:
1) became famous,
2) was asked to turn it into a Broadway play,
3) had financial security.

He was very Sensitive to Loneliness

1) The portrait of male farm life in this novel is accurate — Steinbeck had lived it. He knew his stuff.
2) But he'd always wanted to be a writer. He'd had some books published previously, but it wasn't until "Of Mice and Men" got published in 1937 that he became a success.
3) After a while, however, his own shyness and need for privacy made the pressure of becoming a public figure difficult for him. He wrote, "I just need to get away from being John Steinbeck for a little while."
4) He was acutely sensitive to loneliness, and knew the importance of the comfort and companionship of love.

"Of Mice and Men" keeps getting Banned

"Of Mice and Men" was the 2nd most frequently banned book of the 1990s.
This is why it gets banned lots:

1) Because of the language and the swearing.
2) Because of its portrayal of Crooks, and the innate racism.
3) Because its morality is questionable (prostitution, murder etc).
4) Because of the violence.

It's often thought to be unsuitable for the age group of school students it's taught to.
I can't think why. I mean, they only kill a dog before some guy shoots his best friend in the head...

The dog DID eat Steinbeck's Homework

One more thing you may find useful to impress your teacher with — when he'd written the first half of the book (in pencil, he always wrote in pencil) the dog ate it. Yup, his setter (Toby) shredded it.

But the good news is:

1) he was able to write the first half again from memory.
2) he didn't beat his beloved dog (hey — Carlson would have shot it...).

So you CAN use it as an excuse for late homework.

Sold — one old depressed blind sheepdog with drool...

Steinbeck never expected "Of Mice and Men" to do that well. It was chosen by the 'Book-of-the-Month' Club, guaranteeing it a large audience and big sales. Within just a few weeks of being published, the book sold 117,000 copies. "That's a hell of a lot of books," Steinbeck said.

The World in the 1930s

America was in a right old mess in the 1930s. Financial headaches, economic depression, poverty.
Understanding the social conditions of the time should help you understand just why this novel
became a classic overnight... And you can also look clever in your essays with the stuff too.

The American Economy was a Nightmare

The American Stock Market on Wall Street crashed catastrophically in 1929.
This led to a massive economic depression in the 1930s, when:

1) Increasing mechanisation was driving agricultural labourers off the land.
2) California was filling with official (and unofficial) refugee camps.
3) Drought and over-farming were reducing the amount of fertile land.
4) Owners in states further east such as Oklahoma and Arkansas were going bankrupt and land was repossessed by the banks.
5) Some banks themselves were collapsing. Some bankers committed suicide because they'd lost millions...
6) All of it was worse if you were black — America was still a highly racist, and segregated society.

> This is the American Dream —
>
> "all men are created equal, that they are endowed by their creator with certain unalienable rights, that among these are life, liberty and the pursuit of happiness." (Declaration of Independence, 4th July 1776)
>
> In the depression, this dream was no longer a possibility.

> **Of Mice and Men was first published in 1937.**

The American Dream was Dead

Poverty and starvation stalked California and other stricken states. The migrants were worst off.
There had been no unions to protect the workers. The bosses held on to their own wealth.
The rich stayed rich and the poor stayed poor. The American Dream was dead:

1) There was no more unclaimed land for the poor masses to claim as their own.
2) Striking gold wasn't as easy as it had been.
3) Wages were low so no one could save.
4) Many didn't even find jobs — there was a 30% unemployment rate.

Everyone was suffering, and everyone just wanted to have a better quality of life.

The World was in a Mess

The depression affected Europe economically too. And politically, Europe was slowly descending
into chaos (especially because of the rise in fascism in Germany, Italy and Spain).
In 1937, when Steinbeck wrote "Of Mice and Men":

1) Civil war broke out in Spain in an attempt to suppress fascism.
2) The Nazis were in power in Germany and becoming increasingly repressive — World War Two was coming.

Steinbeck's book isn't about any of these things specifically. But in a world filling increasingly
with chaos and economic depression, here was a story that almost everyone could identify with.
So, unsurprisingly, it sold, and sold, and sold, and sold, and....

Economic nightmares — not if you're a blue monkey...

One ray of sunshine — this book made John Steinbeck an instant success. Although his characters
are depressed and miserable, you can take comfort in the fact that in real life, John Steinbeck's
dream of being a writer came true — he didn't have to shoot anyone in the head for it either...

Section Four — Revision Summary

Okay then — this is the final section in the book. You know what that means — after this, the book'll be over and you'll be free... At least until you've written your essays and stuff... ah well. It could be worse. You could be at work from 9 til 5 every day of your life. Having the soul sucked right out of you. Plenty of time for that I suppose — you've got your whole life ahead of you. For now though, the most important thing is to make sure that you've really understood this book. If you do, you'll be able to write cracking essays about it and get loads of good marks and get a really good 9 til 5 job that will suck the soul out of you. Anyway, you know the drill. Read, rinse and repeat. Marvellous...

1) Where does the novel begin and end?
2) Does the farm seem like a healthy environment for Lennie and George? Explain your answer.
3) Give three reasons why "Of Mice and Men" is a very visual book.
4) Why do you think Steinbeck uses racist language?
5) What is a "Jackson fork"? Choose from the following:
    a)   something Michael Jackson eats monkey poo with,
    b)   a mechanical hayfork,
    c)   not a spoon?
6) What is a "jerkline skinner"?
7) Are "pants rabbits" cute and furry? Why?
8) Are the places mentioned in the book real or fictional?
9) Give three reasons why "Of Mice and Men" keeps getting banned.
10) What part did Steinbeck's dog play in the writing of the novel?
11) What do you think Steinbeck could be saying about the laws of nature in this novel? Write a couple of paragraphs to explain your answer.
12) Write a paragraph explaining how the levels of violence build up through the book.
13) What kind of effect did the 1929 Wall Street Crash have on rural America?
14) Why did it become impossible for people to pursue the American Dream during the economic depression?
15) Why do you think "Of Mice and Men" was so successful when it was published?

AND FINALLY...

Include these Three Things in your Essays

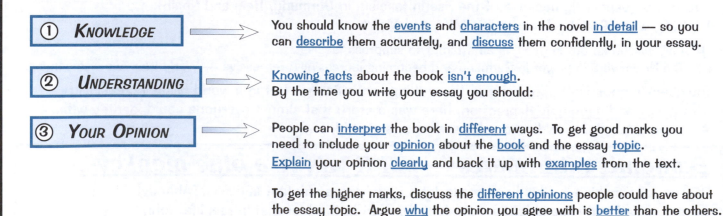

① **KNOWLEDGE** → You should know the events and characters in the novel in detail — so you can describe them accurately, and discuss them confidently, in your essay.

② **UNDERSTANDING** → Knowing facts about the book isn't enough.
By the time you write your essay you should:

③ **YOUR OPINION** → People can interpret the book in different ways. To get good marks you need to include your opinion about the book and the essay topic.
Explain your opinion clearly and back it up with examples from the text.

To get the higher marks, discuss the different opinions people could have about the essay topic. Argue why the opinion you agree with is better than the others. Again, it is really important to support your argument with examples.

The Index

Symbols

117,000 copies 42
1902 42
1930s 43

A

aggressive 18
America 43
American Dream 36, 43
animals 4, 19, 29
anxious 22
Aunt Clara 8, 19, 33
authority 30, 33

B

background stuff 40
bankrupt 43
banned 42
battle of the sexes 33
beans 5
bear 4, 19
big brother 20
Bill Tenner 8, 24, 29
bindle bums 41
bindle stiffs 41
black 11, 23, 34
boasts 26
booby hatch 41
books 23
booze 34
boss 6
bow-legged 41
boxer 22
Broadway play 42
brothels 8, 24, 33
bucking grain 41
bully 23
bum steer 41
bunkhouse 6
burned 41
bus driver 17
bustin' a gut 41

C

cage 37
California 42
Candy 9, 10, 13, 27, 28, 30, 35, 38
Candy's Dog 30
canned 41
cards 38
Carlson 6, 8, 21, 30, 35
cat-house 41
cave 37
chaos 43
childlike 19
chocolate 34
civil war 43
Clara's 8
companionship 26, 34
compensation money 9
conclusion 1
county 41
crack 41

crazy 19
crippled 23
Crooks 10, 11, 29, 35, 38
cruel world 30
crushed 9
cuckoo 19
cultivator 41
Curley 6, 13, 29, 35
Curley's hand 9
Curley's Wife 6, 10, 11, 12, 13, 26, 35, 38
cynical 18

D

dark side 38
dead dog 27
dead dream 27
dead mouse 5
dead puppy 12
dead wife 27
death 37
Declaration of Independence 43
depressed 40
depressing 27, 35, 40
design of the book 40
destructive 20
dialect 41
dog 27, 30, 38
dog ate it 42
dog's life 8, 9
doomed 24, 35
dramatic 40
dreams 9, 13, 18, 26, 35, 36, 37
dress 38
drought 43
dum-dum 11, 19

E

economic depression 43
economy 43
Elm Street 36
enthusiastic 24
essay 1
euchre 41
execution 30

F

failure 35
famous 42
fascism 43
fate 25
fatta the lan' 4, 10
fetish 20, 33, 38
fighting 9, 22
fists 22
flirting 26
floosy 41
flop-house 41

G

Gang aft agley 32
George (pretty much the whole book)
Glove fulla Vaseline 9, 22
Godlike 25
gold 43

Golden Gloves 24
greybacks 41
gut ache 27

H

hands 9, 31
handy 31
hierachy 29, 39
Hitler 43
hoosegow 41
horse 4
horseshoes 23

I

independence 36
inevitable 35, 37
innocence 19, 40
insecure 22
insensitive 21
insults 41
interpreting things 38
introductions (in an essay) 1
introductions 6
irrigation ditch 17

J

jack 41
Jackson fork 41
jailbait 26
jealous 22
jerkline skinner 25, 41

K

ketchup 5
killer 20

L

land 36
language 41
lard 24
laws of nature 40
Lennie (pretty much the whole book)
lice 27
loneliness 34, 42
lonely 22, 23, 34
lynching 37

M

machines 29
machine-gun wielding-goats 39
marriage 34
mechanisation 43
men 33
metaphorically shot in the head 38
metaphors 38
mice 5, 19, 35
middle section 3
mob 29
money 9
morality 42
Mr. Bond 21
mysterious 25

The Index

N

naive 24
names 32
nature 5, 38, 40
nazi 43
Neighbours 39
neurotic 22
nigger 11, 23
nightmare 43
no name 32
noose 30

O

Of Mice and Men 32, 42
old sheep 11
opportunity 36
other stuff 42
over-farming 43

P

pants rabbits 41
parent 20
parental theme 5
pendula 31
pessimistic 17
planning 3
play 40
poison 18
possessions 6, 23
pounding your tail 41
power 23, 25
Prince of the Ranch 25
prison 37
promise 36
puppy 12 (puppies are everywhere...)
purty 7, 41

R

rabbits 4
racism 23, 42
racist 41, 43
rat trap 26
red 38
red dress 17
refugee 43
responsibility 17
restless 22
revenge 13
river 4
Robert Burns 32
Rolf Harris 8
rollercoaster ride 5, 40

S

Salinas Valley 42
schizophrenic 33
sex drive 19
sexes 33
sexual 19, 38
sexuality 33
shots of corn 41
six feet under 40

skinner 25, 41
slang 41
Slim 6, 8, 13, 24, 25, 29, 30, 31, 35
soft 22, 33
soft hair 12
Soledad 32
solitaire 34, 38
spiritual 25
Steinbeck 40, 42
Stephanie 11
stereotype 33
stock market 43
stroking 12, 20, 33, 38
structure 40
stupidity 35
Sunday 12
suspicious 17
Susy's 8, 24, 33
swamper 27, 41
swearing 42

T

tame 19
terrier 4
The Dream 4, 10
titles 32
Toby 42

U

unemployment 43
unhappy 26 (and most of the book)
unsuitable 42

V

vaseline 9, 22, 33
very very lonely 26
violence 42
violent 19, 35

W

wabbits 31
Wall Street 43
warning 5
Weed 4, 8, 12, 17, 32, 38, 40
weird words 41
weirdo 18, 20
Whit 8, 24, 35
whores 34
women 33
World War Two 43

That's All Folks